"Miller is laser focused on confronting the problem that democratic societies fall well short of the longstanding ideals that have informed them. In developing the provocative idea of 'Post-Democracy' to orient us within this situation, Miller advances the study of democracy."
—Jeffrey E. Green, University of Pennsylvania

"Unlike those who say 'Don't vote! It only encourages them,' Caleb Miller does not want us to abandon taking part in political activity, even though he believes it is largely illusory. Should we do this only to continue mourning the absence of effective democracy? Or will our actions from time to time ignite a spark of real possibilities? Miller's rich ambiguity makes us think for ourselves—the best success an author can have."
—Colin Crouch, author of *Post-Democracy* and *Post-Democracy after the Crises*

LIVING UNDER POST-DEMOCRACY

When money equates to power and the system is rigged in favor of wealthy elites, why do we still pretend we are living in a democracy? In *Living under Post-Democracy*, Caleb R. Miller challenges us to admit what we already know: that most of us are effectively powerless over the political decisions that govern our lives. Instead, we should embrace a 'post-democratic' view of politics, one which recognizes the way in which our political institutions fail—both systematically and historically—to live up to our democratic ideals, while also acknowledging our tragic, yet enduring attachment to them both.

Offering a new framework for conceptualizing contemporary citizenship, Miller explores how a post-democratic perspective can help us begin to reorient ourselves in our paradoxical, fractured political landscape. This model of citizenship opens the possibility for a distinctly post-democratic approach to both political participation and political philosophy, treating them not as ways of affecting politics, but as opportunities for therapeutically engaging with the ongoing challenges and inevitable frustrations of post-democratic life.

This book is an excellent addition to courses on democratic theory, as well as introductory courses to political theory.

Caleb R. Miller is a Visiting Fellow at the Ash Center for Democratic Governance and Innovation at the Harvard Kennedy School. He has published in *Constellations*, *Hobbes Studies*, and the *Journal of Political Science Education*. In addition to his work on post-democracy, his research interests include democratic realism, political realism, and the work of Thomas Hobbes. Miller received his PhD from the University of California, Santa Barbara; he currently resides in Somerville, MA with his wife and son.

ROUTLEDGE ADVANCES IN DEMOCRATIC THEORY

Edited by Paulina Tambakaki (University of Westminster), Lasse Thomassen (Queen Mary, University of London) and David Chandler (University of Westminster)

Advisory Board: Amy Allen (Penn State University), Benjamin Barber (City University of New York), Rajeev Bhargava (Centre for the Study of Developing Societies), Fred Dallmayr (University of Notre Dame), John Keane (University of Sydney), James R. Martel (San Francisco State University), Chantal Mouffe (University of Westminster), Davide Panagia (UCLA), Bhikhu Parekh (House of Lords), and Nadia Urbinati (Columbia University)

Democracy is being re-thought almost everywhere today: with the widespread questioning of the rationalist assumptions of classical liberalism, and the implications this has for representational competition; with the Arab Spring, destabilizing many assumptions about the geographic spread of democracy; with the deficits of democracy apparent in the Euro-zone crisis, especially as it affects Greece and Italy; with democracy increasingly understand as a process of social empowerment and equalization, blurring the lines of division between formal and informal spheres; and with growing demands for democracy to be reformulated to include the needs of those currently marginalized or even to include the representation of non-human forms of life with whom we share our planet.

Routledge Advances in Democratic Theory publishes state of the art theoretical reflection on the problems and prospects of democratic theory when many of the traditional categories and concepts are being reworked and rethought in our globalized and complex times.

The series is published in cooperation with the *Centre for the Study of Democracy, University* of Westminster, London, UK.

11. Agonistic Democracy
Rethinking Democratic Institutions in Pluralist Times
Marie Paxton

12. Living under Post-Democracy
Citizenship in Fleetingly Democratic Times
Caleb R. Miller

For more information about this series, please visit: www.routledge.com/Routledge-Advances-in-Democratic-Theory/book-series/RADT

LIVING UNDER POST-DEMOCRACY

Citizenship in Fleetingly Democratic Times

Caleb R. Miller

NEW YORK AND LONDON

First published 2020
by Routledge
52 Vanderbilt Avenue, New York, NY 10017

and by Routledge
2 Park Square, Milton Park, Abingdon, Oxon OX14 4RN

Routledge is an imprint of the Taylor & Francis Group, an informa business

© 2020 Taylor & Francis

The right of Caleb R. Miller to be identified as author of this work has been asserted by him in accordance with sections 77 and 78 of the Copyright, Designs and Patents Act 1988.

All rights reserved. No part of this book may be reprinted or reproduced or utilised in any form or by any electronic, mechanical, or other means, now known or hereafter invented, including photocopying and recording, or in any information storage or retrieval system, without permission in writing from the publishers.

Trademark notice: Product or corporate names may be trademarks or registered trademarks, and are used only for identification and explanation without intent to infringe.

Library of Congress Cataloging-in-Publication Data
Names: Miller, Caleb R., author.
Title: Living under post-democracy : citizenship in fleetingly democratic times / Caleb R. Miller.
Description: New York, NY : Routledge, 2020. |
Series: Routledge advances in democratic theory ; 12 | Includes bibliographical references and index.
Identifiers: LCCN 2019053691 (print) | LCCN 2019053692 (ebook) |
ISBN 9780367322335 (hardback) | ISBN 9780367322342 (paperback) |
ISBN 9780429317446 (ebook) | ISBN 9781000034868 (adobe pdf) |
ISBN 9781000034882 (mobi) | ISBN 9781000034905 (epub)
Subjects: LCSH: Citizenship. | Political participation. | Democracy.
Classification: LCC JF801 .M548 2020 (print) | LCC JF801 (ebook) |
DDC 323.6--DC23
LC record available at https://lccn.loc.gov/2019053691
LC ebook record available at https://lccn.loc.gov/2019053692

ISBN: 978-0-367-32233-5 (hbk)
ISBN: 978-0-367-32234-2 (pbk)
ISBN: 978-0-429-31744-6 (ebk)

Typeset in Bembo
by Taylor & Francis Books

To my wife and son, who make it all worthwhile

CONTENTS

Acknowledgments	*xi*
Preface	*xiii*

1 Introduction   1

A Brief History of Democracy 4
Democracy in Despair 6
Contemporary, Mass "Democracy" 9
Introducing Post-Democracy 11
Plan of the Book 14

2 What is Post-Democracy?   21

Democratic Failure 22
Democratic Values 24
Democratic Sovereignty 26
Democratic Tradition and Culture 28
The Problem of Post-Democracy 33

3 Idealism, Realism, and Acknowledgment   40

Democratic Idealism 41
Inexorable Idealism 45
Democratic Realism 48
Acknowledging Post-Democracy 53

x Contents

4 Post-Democratic Political Philosophy   58

Fear and Loathing under Post-Democracy 59
Philosophy as Therapy 62
Political Philosophy as Therapy 65
Post-Democracy and Pessimism 68
Confronting Post-Democracy 70

5 Post-Democratic Citizenship   76

Post-Democratic Political Domination 77
Hobbesian Inroads into Post-Democratic Philosophy 79
The Subject and the Servant 82
Democratic Hope and Post-Democratic Fear 85
A Post-Democratic Political Logic 88

6 Post-Democratic Participation   97

Three Approaches to (Pseudo-)Political Activity 98
Post-Democracy in Practice 103
The Politics of Post-Democracy 107

7 Conclusion   113

Index   *115*

ACKNOWLEDGMENTS

I am indebted to a host of friends, family, and colleagues, without whom this book would not have been possible. First among them are Andrew Norris, P.E. Digeser, and M. Stephen Weatherford, whose endless support and encouragement, even (or perhaps especially) when skeptical of my position, enabled me to grow both as a writer and scholar in ways that I could have never realized alone. Each read and commented on several early drafts of these chapters, and while all mistakes remain my own, any insight this work offers is in large part due to their thoughtful interventions and the ongoing questions they inspire. To that end, I must also thank Bruce Bimber, Thomas Carlson, Joshua Foa Dienstag, Thomas Hughes, and M. Kent Jennings for their invaluable instruction, commentary, and latent contributions to this book. As this is my first book, I want to further recognize a number of early mentors and exemplars, who, in ways both subtle and profound, contributed to my ability to write this book, including Nancy Armstrong, David Bering-Porter, Chad Cyrenne, Bernard Harcourt, Marissa Guerrero, Bernard Reginster, and Ellen Rooney. In particular, I want to thank Corey D. B. Walker, J. Michael Silverman, and Michael Gottsegen for guiding my first 'serious' scholarly effort over a decade ago, and Benjamin Jewell, for inspiring my initial (and enduring) fascination with politics and political philosophy.

Additionally, I am deeply appreciative for Natalja Mortensen and her early and enthusiastic interest in my work, as well as Paulina Tambakaki, Lasse Thomassen, Charlie Baker, Maire Harris, Olivia Hatt, and the rest of the wonderful team at Routledge, including the two anonymous reviewers who provided such encouraging and helpful comments on earlier drafts. I am also grateful to the University of California Board of Regents, UC Santa Barbara Graduate Division, and the UCSB Department of Political Science for all of their generous financial assistance during the writing of this book.

Finally, I want to thank Marsha and Jeffrey Miro for their endless love and support; Stephen Hall and Paul Miller, for inspiring me to 'ponder the imponderables'; my parents, for always pushing me to be better than I was and giving me the tools to do so; the wonderful people at Handlebar Coffee and Breakfast Culture Club in Santa Barbara, for the additional office space and, quite literally, fueling this project; and, most of all, my wife, for helping me every step of the way, putting up with my anxieties and all the other nonsense that goes into writing a book, and still making me feel like the luckiest person in the whole world.

PREFACE

This is not a happy book, nor is it an optimistic one. Rather, it proceeds from the disheartening assumption that the vast majority of ordinary citizens living in democratic countries are not, in fact, *democratic citizens* at all, at least not according to any tenable interpretation of the concept; that the People—whether directly or through representative bodies, deliberative practices, civic habits, or other means—do not govern themselves, but are governed by others, typically those with more wealth and, hence, more access to and influence over political outcomes. Moreover, it assumes that this state of affairs, one increasingly well-documented by the empirical literature on the subject, will continue, if not grow worse, leading not to democratic reform or revolution or even, necessarily, more explicit manifestations of authoritarianism and oligarchy, but to a perpetual non-democracy under the diaphanous guise of genuine democratic sovereignty. In response to this paradoxical condition—democratic in speech and conviction, non-democratic in practice—this book examines the broader implications of this context for how citizens think of themselves, particularly their relationship to the state and their fellow citizens, as well as their approach to the practice of political philosophy and their involvement in a speciously democratic political culture. The book asks, in short: what is it to be a *post-democratic citizen*?

I hope that my assumptions are wrong. I hope that ordinary citizens are able to establish new and better democratic habits and practices, that they are able to achieve some sufficient level of popular sovereignty and political equality and, whether again or for the first time, truly become democratic citizens, rendering this book an innocuous thought experiment, merely a paranoid artifact of democracy's low-water mark. But I am haunted by the possibility that this will not be the case, that the conversations this book facilitates will need to continue, and that the questions animating our thinking about politics will focus less and

xiv Preface

less on how citizens can influence political outcomes and more on how they can endure them. To that end, I offer this book as a starting point; a miserable one, but one reflective of the state in which we find ourselves and faithful to the desperation it engenders. We can and must do better, but in the event we do not, we should begin here.

1

INTRODUCTION

> The tradition of all dead generations weighs like a nightmare on the brains of the living.
>
> —*Karl Marx,* The 18th Brumaire of Louis Bonaparte

> But I can't sleep, wretched me, I'm being bitten—
>
> —*Aristophanes,* The Clouds

Democratic citizens, Aristotle tells us, distinguish themselves by their participation "in the administration of justice, and in offices;" they are not just ruled, but take part in ruling.[1] In ancient Athens, this required a great deal of dedication on the citizen's part—time, energy, resources—so much so, that, as one historian puts it, "men passed their lives in governing themselves."[2] Obviously, this meant that not all were able to participate, and in addition to the formal exclusion of women, resident aliens, and slaves, this included a general category of laborers, artisans, and merchants which Aristotle called "mechanics." While not legally barred, these "servants of the community" were considered too far removed to truly be citizens, too preoccupied with earning a living to practice the sort of virtues democracy requires.[3] As Aristotle argues, these men should not be confused with real citizens, for

> if they who hold no office are to be deemed citizens, not every citizen can have this virtue of ruling and obeying; for this man is a citizen … The best form of state will not admit them to citizenship; but if they are admitted, then our definition of the virtue of a citizen will not apply to every citizen.[4]

Thus, using the word 'citizen' to describe the mechanic is not only a mistake, but one which dilutes what Aristotle considers essential about the concept, rendering

2 Introduction

democracy a part-time or symbolic activity that demands little to no commitment on the part of the citizen. Additionally, doing so encourages the mechanic to adopt a distorted political self-understanding, one which mistakes the detached passivity of being ruled for the celebrated virtue of a democratic life. In short, confusing ruling oneself with merely being ruled.

No longer organized into sovereign city-states, most tend not to think about democracy in Aristotelian terms. Rather, for almost two centuries now, most of the English-speaking world and Western Europe have relied on representative systems, civic associations, public discourse, or other forms of political activity more appropriate to mass democracy, those intended to allow the mechanics a chance to have their say. Still, there is good reason to doubt whether such practices really are democratic in the way they are described to be, whether they truly offer the opportunity to exercise political influence or merely the appearance of it. There is also the question as to whether citizens themselves are up to the task, whether they may instead be too inexperienced, unknowledgeable, apathetic, or busy to make effective use of the institutions available to them. In either case, even with the comparatively modest expectations for popular government under mass democracy, it seems difficult, if not disingenuous, to describe the vast majority of ordinary citizens as *democratic* citizens, either in the Aristotelian sense or in any other tenable interpretation. Instead, ordinary citizens seem more like mechanics, citizens in name only, those ruled who do not rule. And like them, they seem to share a flawed political self-understanding, one predicated on a basic level of popular sovereignty and political equality that simply does not exist.

These criticisms are hardly new, nor are they unfamiliar. What is new is the extent to which political scientists and other academics now agree on the matter publicly. As one recent scholar exclaims,

> Indeed, just the titles of recent books on the topic—*Disaffected Democracies, Political Disaffection in Contemporary Democracies, Hatred of Democracy, Why We Hate Politics, Democratic Deficit, Don't Vote for the Bastards! It Just Encourages Them, Vanishing Voters, The Confidence Trap, Ruling the Void, The End of Politics, Democracy in Retreat, Democracy in Crisis?, Democracies in Flux, Uncontrollable Societies and Disaffected Individuals, Is Democracy a Lost Cause?* and *Can Democracy be Saved?*—paint a worrying picture of democratic decline.[5]

To that list, we can add *Democracy Disfigured, How Democracies Die, How Democracy Ends, Democracy Incorporated, One Person, No Vote, Undoing the Demos, The People Vs. Democracy, Democracy in Chains, It's Even Worse Than It Looks, Theorizing Democide,* and *Democracy May Not Exist, But We'll Miss It When It's Gone,* as well as a distressing explosion of scholarly interest in the burgeoning rise of illiberal democracy, authoritarianism, and fascism.[6] But one need not be a political scientist to recognize the deep inequalities—political, economic, and otherwise—that pervade contemporary democratic life and prevent ordinary citizens from exercising the sort of collective

Introduction **3**

power indicative of a working democracy. As many as 64% of Americans now believe that their votes do "not matter because of the influence that wealthy individuals and big corporations have over the electoral process," while nearly 31% of Germans, 33% of Canadians, 49% of Americans, 51% of Britons, 52% of Australians, and 80% of French citizens now express little to no trust in their national governments.[7] The sentiments that 'the system is corrupt,' 'politics is a rigged game,' and 'voting doesn't matter' have all become commonplace, and not just among radicals, but among those with otherwise fairly moderate assumptions about how a democratic society should function. Even former U.S. President Jimmy Carter believes that the United States has "become now an oligarchy instead of a democracy."[8] The minimal expectations that representatives serve all their constituents, and not just their donors, or that politicians speak truthfully have become so discredited as to be Pollyannaish, despite being indispensable prerequisites for any sort of conceivable democracy.

And yet, out of optimism, apathy, or a lack of alternatives, these citizens cling to the idea that they still somehow exercise some degree of intentional or meaningful influence over political outcomes. They stay informed, discuss the issues of the day, and continue to involve themselves, all under the presiding, latent assumption that such efforts will eventually affect law and policy. This is in no small part due to both the weight of democratic tradition and the effects of persistently democratic culture; combined, they encourage citizens to treat every imitation or trace of popular sovereignty as proof of their own political power. Even those well aware of just how undemocratic the state really is, continue to speak and act as if it were otherwise, preserving and contributing to a sort of collective democratic inertia, one which leads to a *prima facie* and typically enduring belief in democratic citizenship.

They continue, for example, to treat the state and its decisions as legitimate because they assume it constitutes an expression of popular sovereignty, despite knowing full well just how little the preferences of ordinary citizens factor into those decisions. They think of themselves, by virtue of this specious ability to decide, as being members of a democratic society, even as their firsthand experience of politics regularly puts that ability into question. They imagine that they are responsible to the state, obligated to follow its laws or serve in the military, as well as culpable for its decisions, feeling as if they have to answer for its crimes, all because they continue to believe that 'We, the People' are the state, and the state is them. As such, despite a growing awareness of the political powerlessness of ordinary citizens, democracy inescapably remains the order of the day.

For many, this is a good thing. Our focus on democracy is itself a standing resource for recurrent instances of democratic renewal, rare as they may be. For those of us sympathetic to democratic values (myself included), such an attachment may simply be the natural expression of what we find to be true of or good about politics. Nonetheless, this attachment leaves us in a bind, one which limits our ability and inclination to think of ourselves in non-democratic ways, despite

4 Introduction

the urgent, practical need to do so. This book intends to offer a way out of that bind. Rather than break with democracy completely, which would offer little for a society so indissolubly wedded to it, it seeks to develop a framework for thinking about the broader implications of democracy's absence; in other words, a post-democratic theory of politics.

A Brief History of Democracy

Ordinary citizens have not always thought of themselves in democratic terms. In fact, it is only recently that democracies were even considered desirable. For the ancient Greeks, democracy meant rule by the poor, an anarchic ochlocracy impulsively upending traditional values and plundering the city's wealth for its own immediate gratification. Plato repeatedly criticizes the folly, fickleness, and pandering associated with democratic politics, while even Aristotle, that champion of participatory government, dismisses democracy in favor of *politea*, which includes a healthy dose of oligarchy in order to restrict the masses and produce a stable, middle-class government (one which some might now associate with modern liberal democracy).[9] The Romans, despite their preference for a mixed constitution, distrusted pure democracy, associating it with an unlimited license that erodes all distinction and authority in favor of total equality, a state in which, as Cicero notes, "slaves behave with excessive freedom, wives enjoy the same rights as their husbands, and ... dogs and horses and even asses charge around so freely that one has to stand aside for them in the street."[10] For over a millennia following the collapse of Rome, there was even less interest in democratic politics; with few exceptions (e.g., Marsilius of Padua, William of Ockham), most European thinkers focused on elaborating different theories of papal and monarchical authority. As late as 1787, James Madison argues for adopting the United States Constitution on the basis that it would *prevent* democracy, famously describing democratic governments as those which "have ever been spectacles of turbulence and contention; have ever been found incompatible with personal security or the rights of property, and have in general been as short in their lives as they have been violent in their deaths."[11]

Yet, it was in these debates over the United States' constitution, as well as those in Europe surrounding the French Revolution, that the connotation of the word "democracy" began to change. In the United States, the Anti-Federalists, though losing the fight against ratification, "succeeded in neutralizing the more odious connotations of 'mob rule' ... They also initiated a process by which the rhetorical links between democracy and the ideas of popular sovereignty and political equality were forged."[12] While personally skeptical of democracy, Napoleon built on the foundation laid by the Jacobins to popularize a language of democratic nationalism, advancing the belief that "aristocracy is the spirit of the Old Testament, democracy of the new."[13] During the War of 1812, Americans rallied around democratic rhetoric to distinguish themselves from the monarchic

British, criticizing any element of their political culture perceived to be aristo-cratic.[14] By the Jacksonian Era, the Democratic-Republicans became simply the Democratic Party, no longer interested in emphasizing the republican elitism of its Adamsonian forbears and now fully "committed to the proposition of *vox populi, vox Dei*."[15] With the publication of Tocqueville's two-volume *Democracy in America* in 1840 and 1845, democracy was no longer a dirty word.

Excluding Jean-Jacques Rousseau's early argument for popular sovereignty, it was not until the 19th century that classical liberals like Benjamin Constant, Alexis de Tocqueville, John Stuart Mill, and others began to develop the idea of mass democracy, not because they supported it, but because it seemed inevitable. As such, these early democrats all took efforts to find ways of moderating, if not diminishing popular sovereignty. Constant advocates for a limited level of popular participation, but only to help police the excesses of the state, which, for him, amounted to any-thing beyond protecting individual liberty.[16] Participation for him was not about collective rule, but largely for the moral education of the citizenry, a way of instilling patriotism.[17] Tocqueville, while admiring this sort of civic virtue, also famously warns of "the tyranny of the majority," highlighting the need for authoritative checks on the popular will.[18] And Mill, despite being an early advocate of women's suffrage, calls for plural voting, in which the educated would receive more votes per person than the uneducated masses.[19] Many of their proposals—in particular, their shared commitment to a representative system—would go into effect, often becoming synonymous with democracy itself.

Ultimately, democratic theory would come to dominate Western political thought. Over the next century, the idea of explicitly taking up a non-demo-cratic position (much less an anti-democratic position) was strictly reserved for a dying breed of aristocratic thinkers and virtually impossible for those actively engaged in public life. "No doctrines are advanced as antidemocratic," notes a 1951 UNESCO report, "The accusation of antidemocratic action or attitude is frequently directed against others, but practical politicians and political theorists agree in stressing the democratic element in the institutions they defend and the theories they advocate."[20] Throughout the 20th century, fascists, communists, and liberal democrats would all hold elections, claim and tout 'popular mandates,' and justify foreign interventions on the basis of restoring popular sovereignty and acting in the best interests of the people of Korea, Vietnam, Afghanistan, Iraq, and so on. Now, as Wendy Brown points out,

> We hail democracy to redress Marx's abandonment of the political after his turn from Hegelian thematics (or we say that radical democracy was what was meant by communism all along), we seek to capture democracy for yet-untried purposes and ethoi, we write of "democracy to come," "democracy of the uncounted," "democratizing sovereignty," "democracy workshops," "pluralizing democracy," and more. Berlusconi and Bush, Derrida and Balibar, Italian communists and Hamas—we are all democrats now.[21]

6 Introduction

Regardless of our other political differences, we have come to agree that the democratic society is the good society, and any legitimate political order is unthinkable outside of parameters set by democratic thought.

Democracy in Despair

As democratic values became more and more the norm, social scientists and theorists began exploring the degree to which democratic institutions were able to realize democratic ideals; whether they were, in other words, *truly* democratic. Almost universally, the answer was no, or at least not in a sense that implies popular sovereignty and political equality. Rather, a consensus emerged that wealthy elites, assuming they did not entirely dominate the political process, were at least powerful enough to ensure the protection of class interests and exercise a disproportionate level of control over the broader political agenda.

This occurs first at the level of mass participation itself. Not only are wealthier citizens more likely to have the time and resources to vote, donate to campaigns, and run for office, but they are further incentivized by a system that consistently rewards their preferences while simultaneously discouraging poorer citizens from ever getting involved in the first place. In other words, because they tend to win, wealthier citizens see more value in participation; because they tend to lose, poorer citizens treat it with suspicion and disdain. "Political participation in America is highly stratified by social class, and that stratification has been a feature of political activity for as long as we have had surveys to measure it" Schlozman, Verba, and Brady write, "our major conclusion is the substantial and continuing participatory advantage enjoyed by the well-educated and affluent."[22] And while this has not always been the case in Europe, due in large part to mass mobilization efforts by trade unions and left-wing parties, the decline of these institutions is having an effect, leading to lower rates of participation by the less wealthy and less educated.[23]

More decisively, those with extreme wealth are able to exercise influence over several dimensions of the political process that ordinary citizens are simply unable to access. As Thomas Dye explains, economic elites can produce policy papers through think tanks and foundations; directly influence candidates through substantial campaign donations; lobby through interest groups; influence public opinion through the media; legitimize policy through entrenched institutions; shape policy implementation by influencing bureaucratic offices; and, in the last instance, even affect how policy is evaluated by regulatory boards.[24] Even just *having* wealth gives elites a unique form of power over elected officials. As former American lobbyist Jack Abramoff explains,

> When we would become friendly with an office and they were important to us, and the chief of staff was a competent person, I would say or my staff would say to him or her at some point, "You know, when you're done working on the Hill, we'd very much like you to consider coming to work

for us." Now the moment I said that to them or any of our staff said that to 'em, that was it. *We owned them. And what does that mean? Every request from our office, every request of our clients, everything that we want, they're gonna do. And not only that, they're gonna think of things we can't think of to do.*[25]

In addition to the promise of future wealth, Thomas Mann and Norman Ornstein further explore the degree to which wealth can be used to threaten those who refuse to advance elite interests.

We have had conversations with several incumbents in the Senate up for election in 2012. They say the same thing: they can handle any of the several prospective opponents they might face, but all of them fear a stealth campaign landing behind their lines and spending $20 million on "independent" efforts designed to portray the incumbent as a miscreant and scoundrel who should be behind bars, not serving in the Senate.[26]

In the United States, this culminates in a system where the wealthy decide policy, occasionally disagreeing with one another, but are never seriously challenged by the vast majority of ordinary citizens. As Gilens and Page have recently shown,

When the preferences of economic elites and the stands of organized interest groups are controlled for, the preferences of the average American appear to have only a minuscule, near-zero, statistically non-significant impact upon public policy … To be sure, this does not mean that ordinary citizens always lose out; they fairly often get the policies they favor, but only because those policies happen also to be preferred by the economically-elite citizens who wield the actual influence.[27]

While yet to be so thoroughly demonstrated in Europe, preliminary work suggests that European elites enjoy a somewhat comparable level of political control, with recent scholarship highlighting "the significant decline of democratic choice at the national level" brought on by "the financial industry lobby in Brussels, representing the interests of capital owners."[28] At best, existing democracies appear to facilitate only a narrowly circumscribed degree of popular sovereignty; at worst, they seem to thwart it entirely.

Moreover, ordinary citizens seem quite incapable of doing anything about it. Presumably, an organized, well-informed electorate would be capable of governing itself, but this is precisely what modern democracies seem to lack. Not only are most people deeply uniformed about politics, many of them are also wildly misinformed, acting on patently false information and resistant to new information.[29] Anthony Downs famously describes this as a rational ignorance; citizens with no real ability to influence political affairs have no reason to inform themselves.[30] This ultimately creates a set of conditions where an election is less an opportunity for a

8 Introduction

reasoning public to voice its preference and more the knee-jerk reaction of an unreflective plebiscite. As Christopher Achen and Larry Bartels put it,

> Like medical patients recalling colonoscopies, who forget all but the last few minutes, the voters' assessments of past pain and pleasure are significantly biased by "duration neglect." Their myopia makes retrospective judgments idiosyncratic and often arbitrary ... The result of this kind of voter behavior is that election outcomes are, in an important sense, *random*.[31]

As a result, citizens are effectively unable to use elections as a means of holding politicians accountable, much less to pursue any sort of collective preference.

The decline of associational life, wherein one can make relationships with other members of one's community and learn the skills necessary for political action, has left ordinary citizens at a further disadvantage. "Where once cross-class voluntary federations held sway," notes Theda Skocpol, describing the privatization of political life in the United States,

> national public life is now dominated by professionally managed advocacy groups without chapters or members. And at the state and local levels "voluntary groups" are, more often than not, non-profit institutions through which paid employees deliver services and coordinate occasional volunteer projects.[32]

As Robert Putnam argues in his now classic work, *Bowling Alone*, the connections formed in public life are essential to democratic health; without them, citizens are less inclined to engage themselves or trust one another.[33] In Europe, Francesco Sarracino and Malgorzata Mikucka have shown a similar decline in associational life, as well as a correlative decline in political trust; they note that this decline in trust is "particularly worrying for the democratic future of Europe, *especially* as they are coupled with declining participation in groups and associations."[34] This means not only are democratic citizens living much more 'individualized' lives, but many of them now have a diminished understanding of the problems facing their communities. Among the wealthy, there is also a declining sense of duty to solve them. As Robert Reich warns,

> For without strong attachment and loyalties extending beyond family and friends, [the wealthy] may never develop the habits and attitudes of social responsibility. They will be world citizens, but without accepting or even acknowledging any of the obligations that citizenship in a polity normally implies ... Without a real political community in which to learn, refine, and practice the ideals of justice and fairness, they may find these ideals to be meaningless abstractions.[35]

Without any sort of political community, citizens are simply unable to affect outcomes. As the great John Dewey stresses, an isolated public cannot "use the

organs through which it is supposed to mediate political action and polity";
rather, in their confusion and apathy, the public becomes "eclipsed" by better
organized interests.[36] He explains,

> When the public is as uncertain and obscure as it is today, and hence as
> remote from government, bosses with their political machines fill the
> void between government and public. Who pulls the strings which move
> the bosses and generates power to run the machines is a matter of surmise
> rather than of record, save for an occasional overt scandal.[37]

Without a broader associational life, individual citizens are simply unable to
develop the sort of political consciousness necessary for democratic governance,
much less able to compete with those well-financed and experienced interests
deeply entrenched in power.

Even at the level of public discourse, the public seems unable to enforce basic
norms of respect and truth-telling essential to democratic life.[38] One need not look
far to find evidence of how campaigns, interest groups, and the news media are
able to manipulate and dilute political discourse, transforming what should be
complex conversations into a flurry of soundbites, slogans, and *ad hominem* attacks.
As James Fishkin points out, "As our political process is colonized by the persuasion
industry, as our public dialogue is voiced increasingly in advertising, our system has
undertaken a long journey from Madison to Madison Avenue."[39] As a result, the
Fourth Estate—the newspapers and networks charged with pursuing the truth in
the name of the public interest—has faltered, succumbing to market forces that
support 'infotainment' at the expense of more investigative journalism necessary for
citizens to govern. Robert Entman further explains that "with limited demand for
first-rate journalism, most news organizations cannot afford to supply it, and
because they do not supply it, most Americans have no practical source of the
information necessary to become politically sophisticated."[40] This, coupled with a
rapid growth in other entertainment options, allows citizens to simply 'opt out' of
politics. "Cable television and the Internet have transformed 'politics by default'
into politics by choice," Markus Prior explains, "by their own choice, entertainment fans learn less about politics than they used to and vote less often."[41] Finally,
the Internet, once thought to be a utopian technology for the free exchange of
information and ideas, seems unable to improve political discussion; rather, citizens'
self-selection into heavily curated echo chambers seems to lead to only further
polarization and an increasingly fragmented and hostile public discourse.[42]

Contemporary, Mass "Democracy"

How, then, does contemporary politics work? Written over half a century ago, E.
E. Schattschneider's *The Semisovereign People* still offers perhaps the best account of
contemporary politics, famously describing political activity using the metaphor of

10 Introduction

a street fight.[43] While the fight may begin between two individuals (i.e., elites), they may choose to involve members of the audience in order to change the dynamic of the conflict. By involving some onlookers and excluding others, the fighters can strategically influence the outcome. As Schattschneider puts it, "Private conflicts are taken into public arenas precisely because someone wants to make certain that the power ratio among the private interests most immediately involved shall not prevail."[44] If, for instance, a political actor feels she is unable to prevent a land development project from being approved by the city council, she may invite environmental groups to get involved. Her opponent may then invite even more citizens into the fray with promises of new job opportunities. In this fashion, a conflict can expand to include more and more participants. Yet, the influence exercised by these new participants is largely dependent on the elites at the helm; specifically, the way in which they frame and publicize the issue. In this way, elites largely (if not exclusively) get to decide the available outcomes, deciding precisely what is at stake in the fight, then involving other parties as they see fit. This, in turn, shapes the ordinary citizen's relationship to political activity as reactive, limited, and, above all, perfunctory, a practically mechanical response to directions given by elites, not in the reductive sense that citizens are programmed to think this way or that, but because their opportunities for participation are so deeply managed.

More recent work by Steven Rosenstone and John Mark Hansen, as well as Steven Schier, further supports Schattschneider's analysis. In their book, *Mobilization, Participation, and Democracy in America*, Rosenstone and Hansen explain the process of 'mobilization' whereby elites rally particular segments of the population in order to achieve their goals. Though citizens ultimately decide whether to get involved based on their levels of interest and ability, elites create the context for their involvement through whom they choose to mobilize and when.[45] Schier further describes this as a practice of 'activation,' arguing that this process only gives the illusion of mass participation. He explains that,

> Washington operatives use strategic activation of their people as an example of direct rule by the people, conflating a faction of the public mobilized by an elite with majority opinion. This is not misleading if their people in the aggregate resemble the people. They usually do not.[46]

Instead, consistent with observations offered by Reich, Schattschneider, Rosenstone, and Hansen, he finds that those most often called to participate are those with the time and resources to do so, that is, the wealthy.[47]

This leads Schier to harshly conclude that "America's era of activation is ultimately an era of self-delusion. We trumpet popular participation, yet we have raised the costs of participation and reward those who overcome these costs by activating fragments of the public."[48] Rather, as Skocpol notes, "The most privileged Americans can now organize and contend largely among themselves, without regularly engaging the majority of citizens."[49] Consequently, "early-twenty-first-century Americans live in a diminished democracy, in a much less participatory and more oligarchically managed civic world."[50] In Europe, the matter is further complicated by the European Union, which puts further distance between ordinary citizens and the institutions that govern them. Despite claiming a democratic mandate, the decision-making process in Brussels is routinely criticized for operating in such a way that excludes ordinary citizens, as well as sometimes even their national governments (e.g., Greece 2015).[51]

Under these conditions, ideas about popular sovereignty and political equality appear out of place. Ordinary citizens do not govern, at least not in any meaningful sense, and they certainly do not govern equally. Rather, it seems that the vast majority of them play a primarily *passive* role in politics, assuming they have any role to play at all. This is not to suggest that ordinary citizens do not, from time to time, attempt to play a more active role; simply that, without elite support or co-option, they are almost never able to exercise any significant level of political influence on their own, assuming they even attempt to do so in the first place. To this extent, democratic citizens are not political subjects, but political objects.

Introducing Post-Democracy

Again, all of this is hardly a secret. Most agree that democratic institutions are under threat, others go so far as to suggest that we are witnessing the end of a democratic era— assuming, that is, that democracy ever really existed in the first place. Still, to describe modern, liberal democratic institutions as merely non-democratic fails to capture an essential feature about them: that the threat posed to democracy in these instances is not external (e.g., a brutal dictator, military coup, widespread corruption), but internal in a way that makes it difficult, at times, to identify precisely what is wrong, or *even if* anything is wrong. Elected officials, for instance, though heavily dependent on wealthy donors, must still compete for the popular vote, while representatives are, at least in principle, accountable to their constituencies. Free speech remains protected and citizens are largely allowed to form and join political associations as they see fit. Such practices should act against elite domination and other undemocratic impulses; they do not, yet they still persist as part of a broader political system conceptualized and discussed uniquely in democratic terms. Understood in light of this contradiction, we cannot satisfactorily describe these institutions as either democratic or non-democratic; rather, they must be understood as distinctly *post-democratic*.

Broadly, the term "post-democracy" means "after democracy," and thus can conceivably be used to characterize any institution, state, people, or territory that follows a period of democratic politics. Typically, however, the prefix "post" suggests not only a temporal relationship, but also an essential one, one in which the designated term, despite concluding, continues to play a constitutive role in

12 Introduction

what comes after. For example, a post-war era is not one that simply comes after the war, but one fundamentally marked by both the war's absence and effects. It is, in this sense, unintelligible apart from the war, and persists until some new event or feature comes to take its place in defining that time. Similarly, the postmodern period is that which continues to grapple with the conceptual categories inherited from modernity, just as postpartum names a time defined by the immediate effects of childbirth and post-punk a genre of music exploring the less immediate consequences of the late 1970s punk explosion. The reference to what preceded it—preserved by the "post"—is not arbitrary, but an indication of the dominant or decisive influence still exercised by that element.

Thus, post-democracy names a context which lacks democracy, while still being governed by the ideas and institutions attached to it. As Colin Crouch explains,

> Under this model, while elections certainly exist and can change governments, public electoral debate is a tightly controlled spectacle, managed by rival teams of professionals expert in the techniques of persuasion, and considering a small range of issues selected by those teams. The mass of citizens plays a passive, quiescent, even apathetic part, responding only to the signals given to them. Behind this spectacle of the electoral game, politics is really shaped in private by interaction between elected governments and elites that overwhelmingly represent business interests.[52]

Elections continue to 'work' in the sense that they decide winners and losers, but in a way that consistently produces oligarchic outcomes, functioning as a means of realizing elite preferences, but otherwise unable to assist ordinary citizens in actively influencing policymaking. This is not the result of fraud or voter disenfranchisement (which may still exist, but would be more explicit indicators of non-democracy), but because elections themselves have become (or always were) an inadequate means of exercising political power.

In this sense, post-democracy illuminates a particular kind of democratic failing, one which takes place within self-understood democratic polities that ostensibly still provide opportunities for ordinary citizens to participate in politics. Crouch further elaborates that

> The idea of post-democracy helps us describe situations when boredom, frustration and disillusion have settled in after a democratic moment; when powerful minority interests have become far more active than the mass of ordinary people in making the political system work for them; where political elites have learned how to manage and manipulate popular demands; where people have to be persuaded to vote by top-down publicity campaigns ... One cannot call this kind of politics non- or anti-democratic, because so much of it results from politicians' anxieties about their relations with citizens. At the same time it is difficult to dignify it as democracy itself,

because so many citizens have been reduced to the role of manipulated, passive, rare participants.[53]

Jacques Rancière takes the concept a step further, asserting that post-democracy does not simply imply a managed form of participation, but a manufactured one, thus creating a "paradox that, in the name of democracy, emphasizes the consensual practice of effacing the forms of democratic action."[54] He argues that public opinion polling has largely subsumed the role that should be played by actual citizens, reducing their involvement to little more than spectators. He writes,

> As a regime of opinion, the principle of postdemocracy is to make the troubled and troubling appearance of the people … disappear behind procedures exhaustively presenting the people and its parts and bringing the count of those parts in line with the image of the whole. The utopia of postdemocracy is that of an uninterrupted count that presents the total of 'public opinion' as identical to the body of the people. What in actual fact is this identification of democratic opinion with the system of polls and simulations? It is the absolute removal of the sphere of appearance of the people.[55]

Effectively excluding ordinary citizens from politics, the post-democratic state is then one which can appear democratic without any popular participation at all. It is, as Rancière makes clear,

> the government practice and conceptual legitimization of a democracy after the demos, a democracy that has eliminated the appearance, miscount, and dispute of the people and is thereby reducible to the sole interplay of state mechanisms and combination of social energies and interests … It is an identifying mode, among institutional mechanisms and the allocation of the society's appropriate parts and shares, for making the subject and democracy's own specific action disappear.[56]

In this sense, post-democracy is—to borrow Robert Entman's phrase—a democracy without citizens: a state governed and legitimated by superficially democratic practices that include the People only in such a way as to thwart any real or deliberate exercise of political influence on their part, thus ensuring elite or otherwise authoritarian rule.[57] It is the illusion of democracy, just plausible enough to distort, mystify, and obscure democracy's otherwise conspicuous absence.

Despite a growing interest in post-democracy—or perhaps because of it—there continues to be widespread disagreement over the concept's essential features. This is a relic not only of the various threats to democracy the concept is used to identify, including those posed by economic inequality, international institutions, or even the state itself, but more due to the varying, often disparate

14 Introduction

interpretations of democracy which the concept is used to defend. For example, Crouch turns to post-democracy to describe the collapse of the social democratic welfare state during the neo-liberal privatization of the 1980s, while Richard Rorty uses it to lament the loss of transparency and public accountability resulting from the Global War on Terrorism nearly twenty years later.[58] Rancière goes so far as to suggest that, since democracy is always a form of popular disruption, the modern liberal state is inherently post-democratic simply by virtue of *being a state*.[59]

In addition to (and perhaps as a result of) the absence of a common definition, we further lack a shared sense of the greater implications of post-democracy for the political self-understandings of ordinary citizens, as well as both the reading and writing of political theory. On the one hand, how should the People, unable to exercise political power, understand their relationship to the state, their fellow citizens, and themselves? Bereft of their democratic presumptions, how should they think about concepts like political legitimacy, membership, responsibility, and culpability? On the other hand, how should theorists approach their work in light of the prevailing assumption that the vast majority of one's readers and interlocutors will *not* have any say over how they are governed? What is it to write, not for those with the power to rule or even those who seek it, but simply for the ruled? Moreover, how should such an awareness of powerlessness affect citizens' understanding of their participation in (pseudo-)political practices like voting and dissent? What is it to involve oneself or act when one's actions are insignificant? In sum, how should an awareness of post-democracy influence our understanding of the lived experience of politics and the role of political theory in relation to it? While past thinkers have explored the ways in which post-democratic conditions obstruct the possibility for democratic politics, none have been able to produce a uniquely post-democratic theory of politics, a working framework for our post-democratic present. This book attempts to do just that, not in order to celebrate or defend post-democracy, but to understand it.

Plan of the Book

In hopes of facilitating a more sustained and productive conversation about the concept, Chapter Two begins by developing a general theory of post-democracy. Drawing upon the work of Jacques Rancière, Colin Crouch, Richard Rorty, Jurgen Habermas, Sheldon Wolin, and others, this chapter defines post-democracy as a political context in which failed democratic institutions persist alongside a hegemonic democratic political imaginary. In short, the paradoxical coexistence of a democratic culture and a non-democratic state. This chapter then explores the theoretical implications of the absence of both popular sovereignty and political equality in a context that continues to celebrate them, describing the way in which mass political powerlessness should affect citizens' understandings of legitimacy, membership, responsibility, and culpability.

Chapter Three then explores the ways in which both democratic and post-democratic theorists have approached the problem of mass political powerlessness. In particular, this chapter focuses on two distinct approaches: democratic idealism and democratic realism. While the former treats post-democracy as a practical problem, one to be overcome through political activism and reform, the latter treats it as a conceptual misunderstanding, one predicated on a confused account of what democracy really is. In their exclusive focus on either repairing or explaining democracy's absence, neither approach is able to confront the far-reaching consequences of post-democracy for democratic assumptions about legitimacy, membership, responsibility, and culpability. This then necessitates a new approach, one which more directly confronts the conditions of post-democratic life, treating them as persistent features of contemporary politics.

In light of a post-democratic diagnosis, Chapter Four argues that political philosophy should not be thought of as a means of facilitating the exercise of political power, but a means of working through and coping with a political reality that is completely outside the control of ordinary citizens. As such, under post-democracy, political philosophy assumes an essentially therapeutic character, a means of dealing with the frustration, anxiety, and alienation that emerge from an awareness of ongoing, mass political powerlessness. After first highlighting the cathectic challenges particular to post-democracy, this chapter explores the ways in which past thinkers have understood philosophy as a therapeutic practice, as well as what a therapeutic approach to political philosophy entails. In particular, this chapter examines Jonathan Lear's analysis of the Crow and his resulting concept of radical hope as a foundation for a post-democratic outlook. The chapter ends by contrasting this approach with two other recent responses to political limitation: Joshua Foa Dienstag's pessimism and Jeffrey Green's extrapoliticism.

Chapter Five then puts this therapeutic approach into practice through a post-democratic reading of the work of Thomas Hobbes, one that specifically focuses on his distinction between the subject and the servant. While the subject covenants with others in order to form a commonwealth, the servant is forcibly and violently incorporated into one. This distinction, the chapter argues, parallels the distinction between democratic citizens and self-aware post-democratic citizens under post-democratic conditions. While the former proceeds under the illusion of exercising some control over sovereignty, the latter knows better, preparing the servant for the greater challenges and disappoints of post-democratic life. The chapter ends with a Hobbesian-inspired approach to the questions of legitimacy, membership, responsibility, and culpability that emerge under post-democratic conditions, ultimately arguing for adopting an instrumental relationship to the state and an estranged relationship with one's fellow citizens.

Finally, Chapter Six examines how a post-democratic outlook can inform a practical relationship to the persistent (pseudo-)political activities and habits that continue to structure post-democratic life. After exploring the efforts of Paul

16 Introduction

Kingsnorth's Dark Mountain Project, an environmental group dedicated to mourning the destruction of the planet, this chapter shows how a post-democratic outlook can transform activities like the expression of preference, dissent, and discussion, previously considered political in their own right, into opportunities for therapeutic engagements with the reality of mass political powerlessness. The chapter concludes by addressing the broader political implications of adopting a post-democratic self-conception, ultimately characterizing it as a form of political realism oriented toward overcoming the prejudices of a democratic myopia.

Notes

1 Aristotle 1998, p. 1275a
2 Fustel de Coulanges [1864] 1956, p. 336
3 Aristotle 1998, p. 1278a
4 Aristotle 1998, pp. 1277b–1278a
5 Flinders 2016, p. 182. See Pharr and Putnam 2000, Torcal and Montero 2006, Rancière [2005] 2014, Hay 2007, Norris 2011, O'Rourke 2010, Patterson 2009, Runciman [2013] 2018, Mair 2013, Boggs 2000, Kurlantzick 2013, Papadopoulos 2013, Putnam 2002, Steigler 2012, Mastropaolo 2012, and Della Porta 2013.
6 See Urbinati 2014, Levitsky and Ziblatt 2018, Runciman 2018, Wolin 2008, Anderson 2018, Brown 2015, Mounk 2018, MacLean 2017, Mann and Ornstein 2012, Chou 2013, and Taylor 2019.
7 Jones et al., 2015, p. 30, Pew Research Center 2017.
8 Levine 2015
9 See Plato [1960] 2004, Plato [1955] 2003, and Aristotle 1998.
10 Cicero 2009, p. 31
11 Madison 2012, p. 29
12 Hanson 1985, p. 88
13 Bertault 1916, p. 107. Quoted in Lyons 1994, p. 111.
14 Hanson 1985, ch. 3
15 Hanson 1985, pp. 131, 148
16 Constant [1819] 1988, pp. 326–328. Only a few years earlier, in "Principles of Politics," Constant argues that a King should play this role. See Constant [1815] 1988, pp. 183–194.
17 Constant [1819] 1988, pp. 327–328
18 Tocqueville [1840] 2002, vol. 1, part 2, ch. 7
19 Mill [1861] 2015, pp. 284–300
20 McKeon 1951, p. 522. Quoted in Sartori 1987, p. 3.
21 Brown 2012, p. 45
22 Schlozman et al. 2012, p. 174
23 See Gray and Caul 2000 and Gallego 2007/2008.
24 Dye 2001, Chs. 2–9
25 Quoted in Mann and Ornstein 2012, pp. 68–69, *italics in original*
26 Mann and Ornstein 2012, p. 78
27 Gilens and Page 2014, pp. 575–576
28 Matthijs 2016, p. 414. See also Epp and Borghetto (working paper), Best et al. 2012 and Laurens 2018, as well as the 2016 special issue of *Politics & Society*, "The New Politics of Inequality in Europe," vol. 44, issue 3.
29 See Converse 1964, Kuklinski et al. 2000, Delli Carpini and Keeter 1996, and Zaller 1992.
30 Downs 1957, pp. 244–246, 266–271

31 Achen and Bartels 2016 pp. 175–176, *italics in original*
32 Skocpol 2003, p. 7
33 Putnam 2000, ch. 21
34 Sarracino and Mikucka 2017, p. 425, *italics added*
35 Reich 1992, p. 309
36 Dewey [1927] 1954, pp. 120–121, 134–135
37 Dewey [1927] 1954, p. 120
38 See Cohen 1989, Habermas [1992] 1998, Gutmann and Thompson 1998 and 2004, Fishkin 2009.
39 Fishkin 2009, p. 6
40 Entman 1989, p. 17
41 Prior 2007, p. 256
42 Sunstein 2007, pp. 76–80
43 Schattschneider 1960, pp. 1–3
44 Schattschneider 1960, p. 38
45 Rosenstone and Hansen 2002, p. 6
46 Schier 2000, p. 15
47 Schier 2000, p. 201, Rosenstone and Hansen 2002, pp. 18–19, Schattschneider 1960, pp. 33–35
48 Schier 2000, pp. 40–41
49 Skocpol 2003, p. 178
50 Skocpol 2003, p. 11
51 See also Outhwaite 2014.
52 Crouch 2004, p. 4
53 Crouch 2004, pp. 19–21
54 Rancière [1995] 1999, pp. 101–102
55 Rancière [1995] 1999, p. 103
56 Rancière [1995] 1999, p. 102
57 See Entman 1989.
58 Crouch 2004, pp. 6–11, Rorty 2004
59 Rancière [1995] 1999, pp. 100–101, 108

References

Achen, Christopher H. and Larry Bartels. *Democracy for Realists: Why Elections Do Not Produce Responsive Government*. Princeton, NJ: Princeton UP, 2016.

Anderson, Carol. *One Person, No Vote: How Voter Suppression is Destroying Our Democracy*. New York: Bloomsbury Publishing, 2018.

Aristotle. *Politics*. New York: Cambridge UP, 1998.

Bertault, Jules. *Napoleon in His Own Words*. Chicago: A. C. McClurg and Co., 1916.

Best, Heinrich, György Lengyel, and Luca Lerzichelli. *The Europe of Elites: A Study into the Europeanness of Europe's Political and Economic Elites*. New York: Oxford UP, 2012.

Boggs, Carl. *The End of Politics: Corporate Power and the Decline of the Public Sphere*. New York: Guilford Press, 2000.

Brown, Wendy. "We are All Democrats Now," in *Democracy in What State?*. New York: Columbia UP, 2012.

Brown, Wendy. *Undoing the Demos: Neoliberalism's Stealth Revolution*. Cambridge, MA: MIT Press, 2015.

Chou, Mark. *Theorising Democide: Why and How Democracies Fail*. New York: Palgrave MacMillan, 2013.

Cicero. *The Republic and the Laws*. New York: Oxford UP, 2009.

18 Introduction

Cohen, Joshua. "Deliberation and Democratic Legitimacy," in *The Good Polity: Normative Analysis of the State.* Alan Hamlin and Philip Pettit, eds. New York: Basil Blackwell, 1989.

Constant, Benjamin. "Principles of Politics Applicable To All Representative Governments," in *Political Writings.* Biancamaria Fontana, ed. New York: Cambridge UP, [1815] 1988.

Constant, Benjamin. "The Liberty of the Ancients Compared With That of the Moderns," in *Political Writings.* Biancamaria Fontana, ed. New York: Cambridge UP, [1819] 1988.

Converse, Phillip E. "The Nature of Belief Systems in Mass Publics," in *Ideology and Discontent.* David E. Apter, ed. New York: Free Press of Glencoe, 1964.

Crouch, Colin. *Post-Democracy.* Malden, MA: Polity Press, 2004.

Della Porta, Donatella. *Can Democracy Be Saved?: Participation, Deliberation, and Social Movements.* Malden, MA: Polity Press, 2013.

Delli Carpini, Michael X. and Scott Keeter. *What Americans Know about Politics and Why It Matters.* New Haven, CT: Yale UP, 1996.

Dewey, John. *The Public and Its Problems.* Athens, OH: Swallow Press, [1927] 1954.

Downs, Anthony. *An Economic Theory of Democracy.* New York: Harper and Brothers, 1957.

Dye, Thomas. *Top Down Policymaking.* New York: Chatham House Publishers, 2001.

Entman, Robert M. *Democracy Without Citizens: Media and the Decay of American Politics.* New York: Oxford UP, 1989.

Epp, Derek A. and Enrico Borghetto. "Economic Inequality and Legislative Agendas in Europe." Working paper. <https://enricoborghetto.netlify.com/working_paper/Euro Inequality.pdf> Accessed July 23, 2019.

Fishkin, James. *When the People Speak: Deliberative Democracy and Public Consultation.* New York: Oxford UP, 2009.

Flinders, Matthew. "The Problem with Democracy," *Parliamentary Affairs* 69. 1 (January 2016): 181–203.

Fustel de Coulanges, Numa Denis. *The Ancient City: A Study on the Religion, Laws, and Institutions of Greece and Rome.* New York: Doubleday Anchor Books, [1864] 1956.

Gallego, Aina. "Unequal Political Participation in Europe," *International Journal of Sociology* 37. 4 (Winter 2007/2008): 10–25.

Gilens, Martin and Benjamin I. Page. "Testing Theories of American Politics: Elites, Interest Groups, and Average Citizens," *Perspectives on Politics* 12. 3 (September 2014): 564–581.

Gray, Mark and Miki Caul. "Declining Voter Turnout in Advanced Industrial Democracies, 1950–1997: The Effects of Decline Group Mobilization," *Comparative Political Studies* 33. 9 (November 2000): 1091–1122.

Gutmann, Amy and Dennis Thompson. *Democracy and Disagreement.* Cambridge, MA: Harvard UP, 1998.

Gutmann, Amy and Dennis Thompson. *Why Deliberative Democracy?* Princeton, NJ: Princeton UP, 2004.

Kurlantzick, Joshua. *Democracy in Retreat: The Revolt of the Middle Class and the Worldwide Decline of Representative Government.* New Haven, CT: Yale UP, 2013.

Habermas, Jurgen. *Between Facts and Norms: Contributions to a Discourse Theory of Law and Democracy.* Cambridge, MA: MIT Press, [1992] 1998.

Hanson, Russell. *The Democratic Imagination in America.* Princeton, NJ: Princeton UP, 1985.

Hay, Colin. *Why We Hate Politics.* Malden, MA: Polity Press, 2007.

Jones, R. P., Cox, D., Cooper, B., Lienesch, R. "Anxiety, Nostalgia, Mistrust: Findings from the 2015 American Values Survey." Washington, D.C.: Public Religion Research Institute, 2015. Web. <https://www.prri.org/wp-content/uploads/2015/11/PRRI-AVS-2015-1.pdf> Accessed July 23, 2019.

Kuklinski, James H., Paul J. Quirk, Jennifer Jerit, David Schweider, and Robert F. Rich. "Misinformation and the currency of democratic citizenship," *The Journal of Politics* 62. 3 (2000): 790–816.

Laurens, Sylvain. *Lobbyists and Bureaucrats in Brussels: Capitalism's Brokers*. New York: Routledge, 2018.

Levine, Jon. "Jimmy Carter Tells Oprah America Is No Longer a Democracy, Now an Oligarchy," *Mic* (September 24, 2015). Web. <https://www.mic.com/articles/125813/jimmy-carter-tells-oprah-america-is-no-longer-a-democracy-now-an-oligarchy> Accessed July 23, 2019.

Levitsky, Steven and Daniel Ziblatt. *How Democracies Die*. New York: Crown, 2018.

Lyons, Martyn. *Napoleon Bonaparte and the Legacy of the French Revolution*. New York: St. Martin's Press, 1994.

MacLean, Nancy. *Democracy in Chains: The Deep History of the Radical Right's Stealth Plan for America*. New York: Viking, 2017.

Madison, James. "Federalist 10" in *The Federalist Papers*. Richard Beeman, ed. New York: Penguin, 2012.

Mair, Peter. *Ruling the Void: The Hollowing-Out of Western Democracy*. New York: Verso Press, 2013.

Mann, Thomas E. and Norman J. Ornstein. *It's Even Worse Than It Looks: How the American Constitutional System Collided with the New Politics of Extremism*. New York: Basic Books, 2012.

Mastropaolo, Alfio. *Is Democracy a Lost Cause?: Paradoxes of an Imperfect Invention*. Colchester, UK: ECPR Press, 2012.

Matthijs, Matthias. "The Euro's 'Winner-Take-All' Political Economy: Institutional Choices, Policy Drift, and Diverging Patterns of Inequality," *Politics & Society* 44. 3 (September 2016): 393–422.

McKeon, R. *Democracy in a World of Tensions: A Symposium Prepared by UNESCO*. Chicago: University of Chicago Press, 1951.

Mill, John Stuart. "Considerations on Representative Government," in *On Liberty, Utilitarianism, and Other Essays*. Mark Philip and Frederick Rosen, eds. New York: Oxford UP, [1861] 2015.

Mounk, Yascha. *The People Vs. Democracy: Why Our Freedom is in Danger & How to Save It*. Cambridge, MA: Harvard UP, 2018.

Mounk, Yascha. "America Is Not a Democracy: How the United States Lost The Faith of Its Citizens—And What It Can Do To Win Them Back," *The Atlantic* (March 2018a). Web. <https://www.theatlantic.com/magazine/archive/2018/03/america-is-not-a-democracy/550931/> Accessed July 23, 2019.

Norris, Pippa. *Democratic Deficit: Critical Citizens Revisited*. New York: Cambridge UP, 2011.

O'Rourke, P. J. *Don't Vote, It Just Encourages the Bastards*. New York: Atlantic Monthly Press, 2010.

Outhwaite, William. "The Future of European Democracy," *European Journal of Social Theory* 17. 3 (August 2014): 326–342.

Papadopoulos, Yannis. *Democracy in Crisis?: Politics Governance and Policy*. New York: Palgrave Macmillan, 2013.

Patterson, Thomas E. *The Vanishing Voter: Public Involvement in an Age of Uncertainty*. New York: Knopf Doubleday, 2009.

Pew Research Center. "Few worldwide have a lot of trust in their governments," *Global Attitudes and Trends* (October 12, 2017). Web. <https://www.pewresearch.org/global/

20 Introduction

2017/10/16/many-unhappy-with-current-political-system/pg_2017-10-16_global-dem ocracy_1-03/> Accessed July 23, 2019.

Pharr, Susan J. and Robert D. Putnam. *Disaffected Democracies: What's Troubling the Trilateral Countries?* Princeton, NJ: Princeton UP, 2000.

Plato. *The Republic.* New York: Penguin, [1955] 2003.

Plato. *Gorgias.* New York: Penguin, [1960] 2004.

Prior, Markus. *Post-Broadcast Democracy.* New York: Cambridge UP, 2007.

Putnam, Robert. *Bowling Alone: The Collapse and Revival of American Community.* New York: Simon and Schuster, 2000.

Putnam, Robert. *Democracies in Flux: The Evolution of Social Capital in Contemporary Society.* New York: Oxford UP, 2002.

Rancière, Jacques. *Dis-agreement: Politics and Philosophy.* Minneapolis, MN: University of Minnesota Press, [1995] 1999.

Rancière, Jacques. *Hatred of Democracy.* New York: Verso Press, [2005] 2014.

Reich, Robert. *The Work of Nations: Preparing Ourselves for 21st Century Capitalism.* New York. Vintage Press, 1992.

Rorty, Richard. "Post-Democracy: Richard Rorty on Anti-terrorism and the National Security State," *London Review of Books* 26. 7 (April 1, 2004): 10–11.

Rosenstone, Steven and John Mark Hansen. *Mobilization, Participation, and Democracy in America.* New York: Pearson, 2002.

Runciman, David. *The Confidence Trap: A History of Democracy in Crisis from World War I to the Present.* Princeton, NJ: Princeton UP, [2013] 2018.

Runciman, David. *How Democracy Ends.* New York: Basic Books, 2018.

Sarracino, Francesco and Malgorzata Mikucka. "Social Capital in Europe from 1990 to 2012: Trends and Convergence," *Social Indicators Research* 131. 1 (March 2017): 407–432.

Sartori, Giovanni. *The Theory of Democracy Revisited.* Chatham, NJ: Chatham House Publishers, 1987.

Schattschneider, E. E. *The Semisovereign People: A Realist's view of Democracy in America.* New York: Holt, Rhinehart, and Winston, 1960.

Schier, Steven. *By Invitation Only: The Rise of Exclusivist Politics in the United States.* Pittsburgh, PA: University of Pittsburgh Press, 2000.

Schlozman, Kay, Sidney Verba, and Henry Brady. *The Unheavenly Chorus: Unequal Political Voice and the Broken Promise of American Democracy.* Princeton, NJ: Princeton UP, 2012.

Skocpol, Theda. *Diminished Democracy: From Membership to Management in American Life.* Norman, OK: University of Oklahoma Press, 2003.

Steigler, Bernard. *Uncontrollable Societies of Disaffected Individuals.* New York: Wiley, 2012.

Sunstein, Cass. *Republic.com 2.0.* Princeton, NJ: Princeton UP, 2007.

Taylor, Astra. *Democracy May Not Exist, But We'll Miss It When It's Gone.* New York: Metropolitan Books, 2019.

Tocqueville, Alexis de. *Democracy in America.* Chicago: University of Chicago Press, [1840] 2002.

Torcal, Mariano and José Ramón Montero. *Political Disaffection in Contemporary Democracies: Social Capital, Institutions, and Politics.* New York: Routledge Press, 2006.

Urbinati, Nadia. *Democracy Disfigured: Opinion, Truth, and The People.* Cambridge, MA: Harvard UP, 2014.

Wolin, Sheldon S. *Democracy Incorporated: Managed Democracy and the Specter of Inverted Totalitarianism.* Princeton, NJ: Princeton UP, 2008.

Zaller, John. *The Nature and Origin of Mass Opinion.* New York: Cambridge UP, 1992.

2

WHAT IS POST-DEMOCRACY?

The term "post-democracy" first appears in 1992, when French philosopher Jacques Rancière uses it to criticize liberal democracy as the "non-conflicted rule of experts"; by 1995, he is using the term to describe modern forms of mass political participation as inauthentic and simulated.[1] In 2001, Sheldon Wolin ends his mammoth study of Tocquevillian thought with a chapter entitled "Postdemocracy," in which he highlights the enduring relevance of Tocqueville's warnings concerning 'democratic despotism' and the dangers of an overly-privatized existence.[2] A year earlier, British sociologist Colin Crouch writes *Why Post-Democracy?*, a pamphlet that becomes the basis for his 2004 book, entitled simply *Post-Democracy*.[3] In it, he explores how the pursuit of elite interests, the privatization of public goods, and civic complacency work together to substantially weaken democratic institutions. Two more pieces are published on the topic in 2004, both by Americans. The first, by philosopher Richard Rorty in the *London Review of Books* (also titled, at the request of his editors, "Post-Democracy"), warns against the unchecked power exercised by national security agencies in the wake of 9/11.[4] The second, by foreign policy expert John Fonte in *The National Interest*, criticizes the increasing threat posed to national sovereignty by supranational organizations like the United Nations, World Bank, and International Criminal Court.[5] Remarkably, none of these works reference one another.

Over the next decade, the concept gains further popularity among European social scientists, particularly environmental policy researchers, who use it to describe the disproportionate political power of transnational corporations over local, grassroots activists.[6] In 2012, Jurgen Habermas joins a growing chorus of those designating the European Union as a form of 'post-democratic sovereignty.'[7] Three years later, the first workshop on post-democracy is held in North America at Brown University.[8] Alongside discussions of democratic deficits and

22 What is Post-Democracy?

authoritarian populism, illiberal democracies and oligarchic billionaires, the idea of post-democracy is now being used by scholars, journalists, activists, and ordinary citizens to express the widespread belief that democratic institutions are at risk, perhaps even in historical decline. But what are they really saying when they refer to political institutions as post-democratic? Beyond criticizing democratic shortcomings, are they really saying anything at all?

Despite its prevalence, there is little agreement—or even sustained discussion, for that matter—as to what exactly post-democracy is. Outside of the disparate accounts offered by Crouch and Rancière, the term is often used as if it were self-explanatory, meaning simply 'not democratic anymore.' But why describe a state or institution as post-democratic rather than, say, oligarchic, authoritarian, post-political, or even just non-democratic? What does it imply? Why is it significant? Ultimately, what value does the concept hold for us? In this chapter, we explore the immediate, theoretical implications of a post-democratic diagnosis by first developing a general definition of post-democracy, one able to account for the diversity of interpretations imposed on it, then by identifying a unique set of conceptual problems to which any post-democratic theory of politics must respond. This set of problems revolves chiefly around the question of political powerlessness within a context structured by a hegemonic democratic political imaginary. Specifically, how can we think about systemic and enduring political insignificance in a theoretical context that refuses to admit alternatives to democratic thought? What does it mean to be uniquely post-democratic?

Democratic Failure

Post-democracy begins with the basic premise that democratic institutions are failing or have failed. Rancière introduces the term to criticize manufactured forms of mass participation designed to protect elite interests under the guise of a liberal–capitalist consensus.[9] In particular, he attacks the regime of public opinion, noting how the transformation of actual political disputes into statistical or empirical questions intended for experts removes any space for the People to appear, effectively excising them from politics.[10] For example, if a respected polling firm conducts research into whether citizens are for or against some issue, then there becomes no need for any particular citizen to voice an opinion, especially if that opinion would fall outside the bounds of being simply 'for' or 'against;' after all, the poll already tells us what the People think. For Crouch and Wolin, the situation is somewhat less dire: the People have not been replaced entirely, but now play the role of political consumers rather than participants, with elected officials "more resembling shopkeepers than rulers, anxiously seeking to discover what their 'customers' want in order to stay in business."[11] Wolin describes this as a form of "consumer sovereignty ... benign, power transmuted into solicitude, popular sovereignty into consumerism, mutuality into mutual funds, and the democracy of citizens into shareholder democracy."[12] This is not to suggest, however, that the public gets what it really wants; as Crouch notes, the political world then makes its own response to the unattractive and subservient position in which these changes threaten to place it … [having] recourse to the well-known techniques of contemporary political manipulation, which give it all the advantages of discovering the public's views with the latter being able to take control of the process for itself. It also imitates the methods of … show business and the marketing of goods.[13]

For Habermas and Fonte, it is a matter of national sovereignty. Fonte argues that international organizations like the U.N. or I.C.C. inherently deprive citizens of the possibility of governing themselves, while Habermas worries that Europeans lack the pan-European political consciousness necessary to democratize the E.U., describing, at present, "an asymmetry between the democratic participation of the *peoples* in what their governments 'obtain' for them on the, as they see it, far-off Brussels stage and the indifference, even apathy, of EU *citizens* regarding the decision of their parliament in Strasbourg."[14] For Rorty, post-democracy describes the way in which issues of national security have begun to overdetermine policymaking, gradually displacing the traditional role played by liberal democratic institutions. "In the US and in many of the EU countries," he writes, "an elite has come to believe that it cannot carry out its mission of providing national security if its preparations are carried out in public … Further attacks are likely to persuade those elites that they must destroy democracy in order to save it."[15]

Each of these thinkers highlight, not explicit instances of democratic failure (e.g., a military coup, foreign invasion, fraudulent election) but instances in which ostensibly democratic institutions fail to live up to democratic values, but persist nevertheless. As Crouch makes clear, "virtually all the formal components of democracy survive within post-democracy."[16] In Rancière's case, for example, it is not that elections or public opinion polls have disappeared, but that they have suddenly become tools of elite domination, rendering them marginal and lifeless. These institutions continue to play a major, if not the central role in political life, even among those skeptical of their democratic credentials. Similarly with Habermas, the E.U.'s lack of democratic legitimacy has not inhibited its ability to exercise power, nor has the growing power of national defense and intelligence organizations, in Rorty's account, made liberal democratic institutions fade away altogether. The failure, then, is not fatal, but degenerative, a condition in which the afflicted institutions remain, but as hollow shells of their former (or imagined) selves. In other words, post-democracy requires that democratic institutions that were or were once thought to be democratic have diminished, not in size, scope, or number, but in character. It is the electoral system that once produced popular, qualified candidates that were committed to their constituents, but now only furnishes barely tolerable, 'electable' ones; the open, public discourse intended to reach well-reasoned, un-coerced results, but now primarily breeding misinformation, hostility, and suspicion; the national association with a

24 What is Post-Democracy?

long, vibrant tradition of chapter-driven efforts and initiatives, now managed like a professional lobby and dependent on its membership solely for donations; and the representative body so indebted to its donor class that ordinary citizens must now look to willing oligarchs to save them.

Democratic Values

Of course, there will inevitably be some disagreement as to precisely when a set of democratic institutions have failed, but such disagreement is inherent in the concept of democracy itself. As Selen Ercan and Jean-Paul Gagnon point out,

> Democracy is an essentially contested concept. The word is prefaced by over 500 adjectives (see Gagnon et al. 2014), such as liberal, representative, deliberative, feminist, and radical ... So, what may seem perfectly fine from a liberal electoral perspective can easily be defined as a crisis of democracy when seen from an alternative perspective of democracy.[17]

In order to accommodate the considerable diversity of available interpretations, a general theory of post-democracy requires an equally general theory of democracy, understood not in terms of any particular set of institutions, but only in its pursuit of popular sovereignty and political equality. These two values give us a substantive understanding of democracy that, while inclusive enough to account for most diagnoses of post-democracy, are also discriminating enough to rule out certain interpretations of democracy that would seem to render any such diagnosis impossible.

Why these two values? Popular sovereignty, to begin, is absolutely essential; the idea of democracy is almost unthinkable without it. The ancient Greek *dēmokratíā* translates literally to "rule by the People," which is not to suggest that popular sovereignty implies total democracy to the exclusion, say, of mixed constitutions or other, more explicitly non-democratic institutions (e.g., U.S. Supreme Court, federalism), but simply that any democratic government must privilege opportunities for meaningful, mass political participation. This, moreover, does not mean that the People always rule well. They may routinely, if not consistently, make poor decisions, either as a result of being tricked or entirely of their own volition. The essential feature is just that there is some mechanism by which the People can exercise their political voice.

While popular sovereignty expresses the People's right to rule, political equality stipulates they are able to rule equally, barring political hierarchies based on class, race, gender, or any other distinction that unnecessarily or arbitrarily divides the People in their collective capacity to exercise political power. This, of course, raises the question of *who* exactly constitutes the People. For instance, despite Pericles declaring that Athens "is called a democracy because power is in the hands not of a minority but of the whole people," we know that the ancient

Athenians systematically excluded women, foreigners, and slaves from politics.[18] While this may have fit with the Periclean understanding of who makes up the *demos*, it would not fit the contemporary liberal interpretation, which assumes that women and naturalized foreigners should have political rights and that slavery, of course, should be abolished. Still, both the ancient Athenian and the liberal would agree on excluding children from politics, while future generations may have a more radically inclusive understanding of *universal* suffrage. The decisive question, then, is whether those who are broadly understood, socio-historically speaking, to deserve political rights actually *do* have the ability to exercise political influence at a level similar to other private citizens.[19] While all but total, direct democracies will have elected officials or others who are able to exercise substantially more power, the private individuals that make up the People must, by and large, have similar opportunities to participate in political decision-making. This means that elected officials must remain free from forms of political influence unavailable to ordinary citizens, such as the sort of direct access purchased with substantial campaign donations. Even if everyone can vote, voting may become an insignificant or irrelevant means of exercising influence if some citizens have infinitely more power than others, upending the vote's ability to facilitate popular sovereignty.

This minimal theory of democracy, however, would still preclude those interpretations that dismiss the significance or relevance of either popular sovereignty or political equality, forgoing the democratic pretense that otherwise defines post-democracy. Such theories are, in a sense, resistant to post-democratic diagnoses, if only because their interpretations of democracy already seem to account for the absence of any genuine democracy. Take, for instance, Joseph Schumpeter's democratic realism and Jeffrey Green's plebiscitary democracy. In Schumpeter's case, he argues that popular sovereignty is a myth and "democracy means only that the people have the opportunity of accepting or refusing the men who are to rule them."[20] Similarly, Green argues that contemporary liberal democracies are marked by so much political inequality as to call for a tiered conception of citizenship, reminiscent of formal Roman class structures, in which the mass of ordinary citizens inhabit second-class civic structures.[21] Both may be right, but a general theory of post-democracy depends on an initial model of democracy robust enough that it can fail and still *appear* democratic. For instance, a Schumpetarian post-democracy would imply the move from elite competition to non-competitive elections, essentially reducing it to a single-party state, while a plebiscitary post-democracy would be one in which the masses are not simply at a disadvantage, but one in which they have been excluded entirely, again more akin to an explicitly authoritarian regime. In either case, the model of democracy already resembles post-democracy to such a degree that a further post-democratic designation would be redundant. This is why a minimal commitment to substantive democracy remains essential to the concept. Without it, we miss the kind of failure particular to post-democracy: not a

26 What is Post-Democracy?

kind of institutional collapse, but rather a hollowing out that dissolves what made, or was intended to make, these institutions valuable *from a democratic perspective*, that is, their ability to realize popular sovereignty and political equality.

Democratic Sovereignty

Similarly, post-democracy further depends on a minimal understanding of political activity as that which is able and intended to influence sovereign decision-making. Otherwise, there may be confusion over how a society, despite having certain democratic or egalitarian features, fails to be democratic in a political sense, that is, fails to achieve popular *sovereignty*. Sovereignty, as Jean Bodin tells us, is that "most high, absolute, and perpetuall [sic] power over the citisens [sic] and subiects [sic] in a Commonweale."[22] As Thomas Hobbes makes clear, this power primarily depends on having recourse to supreme and overwhelming violence as a means of enforcing laws and commands; without it, sovereign decisions would hardly be "most high" and "absolute."[23] Such requirements lead Max Weber to define the state as a "human community which (successfully) lays claim to the monopoly of legitimate physical violence within a certain territory," explaining that "violence is, of course, not the normal or sole means used by the state … But it is the means specific to the state."[24] Carl Schmitt further highlights the ability to name public enemies and declare war, "thereby publicly disposing of the lives of men," as the essence of the political.[25] He, like Weber, notes that other associations below the state may still exercise legitimate forms of violence (e.g., paramilitary groups, counter-protestors, "Red Guards"), but the state is the decisive *political* entity to the extent that it is able to authoritatively legitimate or de-legitimate instances of violence.[26] Politics, then, is the practice of managing legitimate violence. What is law-making, after all, but the act of encouraging or prohibiting particular actions or behaviors through the threat of legitimate violence?

Legitimate violence separates politics from all other forms of social activity in its ability to force action and behavior. This gives political power a kind of essential character that distinguishes it both from informal, non-decisive "political" activity (e.g., protesting, signing petitions, visiting political websites, and forwarding political emails) and a host of other activities broadly intended to influence social norms and behavior, but without using recourse to sovereign power (e.g., corporate boycotts, public awareness campaigns, "Cancel culture").[27] The problem in each case is that treating these activities as comparable to more traditional political activities (e.g., elections, referendums, law-making, court decisions) dilutes politics' intrinsic connection to sovereign power, that is, the legitimate use of violence, losing precisely what makes it both unique and sacred in relation to other forms of social activity and further opening the possibility that almost *anything* could be considered political. As such, a general theory of post-democracy requires this minimal understanding of politics as a condition of possibility for making a post-democratic diagnosis. Without it, the People's ability to protest, boycott, or petition would qualify that society as democratic, even if its electoral system or public discourse would not, rendering the sorts of post-democratic critiques already surveyed incoherent. Despite their often disparate targets, Rancière, Crouch, and others agree that post-democracy describes the non-democratic character of ostensibly democratic regimes, not the total cessation of social activity within that regime, which all still tolerate private forms of collective action. In fact, this toleration would seem to constitute one of its essential features, again distinguishing it from more explicitly authoritarian regimes. To equate protest or petition with referendums and elections, not to mention more banal practices like displaying a political bumper sticker or posting about politics on social media, only further mystifies the power imbalance at the heart of contemporary liberal democracies, a system which invites all to speak, but listens solely to the few.

For Rancière, Slavoj Zizek, Chantal Mouffe, and others, post-democracy is also post-political to the extent that elite consensus forecloses the possibility for pursuing alternatives to liberal capitalism, making it a kind of pseudo-politics that focuses on 'subpolitical' issues or 'life politics' (e.g., questions of identity politics, the 'culture wars' in the United States) at the expense of more significant issues related to class and exploitation.[28] Similarly, Stephen Welch uses the term 'hyper-democracy' to describe a context in which an overabundance of these sort of 'subpolitical' concerns paralyzes the People's ability to govern, whether on issues of class or any other.[29] On the one hand, the idea of post-politics directs our attention to one possible consequence of post-democracy, that political possibility, as a whole, would become limited. On the other, as Crouch makes clear, a theory of hyper-democracy would be perfectly consistent with a theory of post-democracy. He writes,

> When there is very little real debate over major policy directions (a fundamental characteristic of post-democracy), politicians start exploring every little avenue they can in order to claim that they have found a difference from their opponents—anything from each other's personal morality to the desirability of particular medical treatments or ways of teaching children to read. This leads to an intrusion of politics—whether democratic or not— into areas with which it is not well equipped to deal.[30]

In this way, hyper-democracy can be read as a symptom of post-democracy, a response to the absence of meaningful political possibilities.

Yet, by no means is the cessation of politics a necessary consequence of post-democracy, nor is hyper-democracy necessarily a symptom. *Contra* the idea of post-politics, elites can still engage in political conflicts that, while not revolutionary, may prove more significant than criticisms of 'subpolitics' or 'life politics' would lead us to believe.[31] For example, states may choose to limit illiberal legislation (e.g., 'bathroom laws') in order to avoid missing out on lucrative conference and athletic contracts, while cities may push for more

28 What is Post-Democracy?

progressive social policies in order to attract new businesses. Again, these conflicts cannot be qualified as the People ruling in any sense, but that does not mean that the outcomes of these conflicts cannot sometimes be in the People's interest. Additionally, a post-democratic state need not be hyper-democratic; in fact, there is no reason why it could not be largely apolitical, as long as citizens still revered democratic practices and values. Ultimately, while insightful, both concepts draw our attention away from the need to rethink the citizen's relationship to the state. This is especially true in the case of 'hyper-democracy.' Part of the problem may be overpoliticization, but in identifying democracy as the cause, a hyper-democratic diagnosis further directs our attention away from the urgent conceptual and evaluative questions that emerge from a *loss* of democratic citizenship rather than its overextension.

Finally, a general theory of post-democracy does not imply the prior existence of any real or historical democracy, only the ongoing role played by democratic ideas within it. Such an interpretation puts us in conflict with Crouch, who argues that post-democracy necessarily follows a maximally democratic moment. He identifies this "democratic moment around the mid-point of the twentieth century: slightly before the Second World War in North America and Scandinavia; soon after it for many others" as one in which "a certain social compromise was reached between capitalist business interests and working people."[32] Yet, such a historical commitment unnecessarily invites the criticism, like that of James Martel, that democracy has never truly existed in the first place. Since even the Keynesian compromises of post-war era were not fully democratic, one could argue that a real, modern democracy has never actually existed, making post-democracy itself a misnomer.[33] But whether a modern democracy has ever *actually* existed is beside the point. What is decisive for a post-democratic diagnosis is not a society's real history, but the history of its ideas: whether democratic values have played and continue to play the authoritative role in that society's political imaginary, meaning that democracy is not only considered good, but an essential element of the good, requiring that the state strive to at least *appear* democratic. This appearance may be in bad faith, an active deception by a political elite who know better, but it may also be enacted with a mistaken sincerity, an earnest effort by noble statesmen and activists who think of themselves as realizing the People's will, even if they are not.[34] In the end, the question is whether this appearance is successful enough that individuals are able to reconcile their relationship to the state within a broader, democratic tradition and culture. It is to this ongoing role played by this tradition and culture to which we now turn.

Democratic Tradition and Culture

As Rancière makes clear, "postdemocracy ... should not be understood as the state of a democracy sadly surrendering its hopes or happily divested of its illusions."[35] Rather, a society is *post*-democratic to the extent that it continues to grapple collectively with the theoretical and normative implications of democratic thought. Despite failing or failed democratic institutions, it continues to predominantly understand itself as a democracy, tending to conceptualize, discuss, and judge politics and the state primarily, if not exclusively, in democratic terms. In this sense, post-democracy depends on a persistent, collective faith in both democratic values and, paradoxically, the democratic legitimacy (or potential) of its institutions.

This faith is sustained, first, by long-standing traditions—intellectual, practical, and popular—that promote the value of democratic ideals and encourage citizens to think of themselves as *democratic* citizens. There are well-established electoral systems, built upon written constitutions or other historical agreements, with widespread suffrage; schools of democratic political thought; historical narratives of democratic progress; deep-rooted civic associations; perennial literary themes; revered heroes; pedagogical principles; sacred holidays; quotes engraved on marble; and songs known by heart. These traditions, while sometimes critical of the state, largely support the belief that the state has always been essentially democratic and, moreover, will remain so. Even those moments that would seem to highlight the state's previous democratic shortcomings (e.g., limited suffrage, periods of corruption) are recuperated into a grand story of democratic development, giving the impression of a democratic spirit or essence that guarantees a democratic future.

Furthermore, there also exist a robust set of cultural practices that work to reinforce a shared perception of democratic citizenship. For example, candidates for office characterize themselves as representatives of the People. Staying informed and voting are considered civic duties, with the presumption that non-participation disqualifies individuals from complaining about political outcomes. The media stresses the decisive import of how citizens think and feel (e.g., public opinion polling, electability, Twitter, "man on the street" interviews). Citizens default to 'majority rule' when collectively making private or informal decisions. Schoolchildren hold class elections and accompany their parents to vote. Everyday discussions about politics presuppose that a certain degree of sovereign power is at stake, that it matters *politically* how an individual feels about a particular issue or candidate, or even how they might do things differently themselves. All these elements work together to envelop individuals in a blanket of democratic conventions, habits, and assumptions that are often inseparable from their broader experience of social life. In short, to be a part of community life is to behave *as if* one were a democratic citizen.

These traditions and habits thus ensure not only that democratic values retain a privileged position within post-democratic society, but also that the state, by virtue of its association with these traditions and habits, retains an image of democratic legitimacy. In promoting this image, they play an essential ideological function, both in the sense of contributing to a broad form of false consciousness, but also in providing for the ideological fantasy of democratic citizenship. On the

30 What is Post-Democracy?

level of false consciousness, these traditions and habits succeed in convincing the vast majority of the population that the state is sufficiently democratic, despite qualitative and quantitative evidence to the contrary. This is in part due to the ubiquity of such traditions and habits, the degree to which they are woven within the fabric of everyday life, but also, as with most complicated or uncomfortable questions, that most people prefer not to think about it. As such, most individuals tend to accept, if not vigorously defend, the seemingly obvious position that their society is democratic. If this were not the case—if the People, as a whole, believed democratic institutions had failed—it would be unclear how the democratic political culture surrounding post-democracy could persist, as well as why it would be of any use. In other words, who would the lie be for? Why pretend? A completely self-aware post-democratic society would end up finding new ways of collectively conceptualizing their politics. They would no longer need to default to 'this-democracy' or 'that-democracy,' but instead adopt a more robust oligarchic or authoritarian political imaginary. In short, it would cease to be post-democratic, and become what it otherwise is. Post-democracy resists being classified simply as non-democracy, oligarchy, or authoritarianism precisely because so much of its self-conception remains intractably indebted to this omnipresent sense of democratic identity and inheritance, faithfully maintained and reproduced by its citizenry.

On another level, for those aware enough of post-democratic conditions to be skeptical of the state's claims of democratic legitimacy, these traditions and habits enable them to continue on *as if* they were still democratic citizens. Here, Zizek's description of ideological fantasy is deeply instructive. Rather than functioning as a form of false consciousness, Zizek argues that ideology works by enabling individuals to avoid confronting the otherwise obvious violence, inequality, and injustice that functions as the basis of their society. He writes,

> Ideology is not a dreamlike illusion that we build to escape insupportable reality; in its basic dimension it is a fantasy-construction which serves as a support for our "reality" itself: an "illusion" which structures our effective, real, social relations and thereby masks some insupportable, real, impossible kernel ... The function of ideology is not to offer us a point of escape from our reality but to offer us the social reality itself as an escape from some traumatic real kernel.[36]

In other words, ideology is not what prevents individuals from discovering that democracy is failing or has failed, as if to shield them from some horrible secret, but what enables them to avoid addressing the broader implications of this realization; namely, by encouraging them to participate in a social reality wherein democracy is presumed alive and well. As Zizek explains,

> What we call "social reality" is in the last resort an ethical construction; it is supported by a certain *as if* (we act *as if* we believe in the almightiness of

bureaucracy, *as if* the President incarnates the Will of the People, *as if* the Party expresses the objective interest of the working class ...). As soon as the belief (which, let us remind ourselves again, is definitely not to be conceived at a "psychological" level: it is embodied, materialized, in the effective functioning of the social field) is lost, the very texture of the social field disintegrates.[37]

Here, the description of belief as "embodied" and "materialized" is critical. The belief, say, that "the President incarnates the Will of the People," is not something that everyone readily accepts as a rational or true proposition; many will dismiss the statement as questionable, if not ridiculous. Yet, despite not having the status of a psychological belief, this 'belief' continues to function on the level of practice. Thus, despite knowing that "the President is a crook, just like all the other presidents," an individual may continue to vote in the election and encourage others to do so; discuss the President's actions as if he should be expressing the People's will; show deference and respect toward the office of the presidency; look forward to a better President that will express the People's will; or otherwise act *as if* the presidency has anything to do with popular sovereignty. Without these sorts of ongoing practices and habits, democracy would lack any substance at all, regardless of whether citizens *believed* in democracy or not. In this sense, practice plays the decisive role, contributing to a broader social reality in which the People continue to act *as if* they govern, even if, as individuals, they know better.

In fact, as Zizek makes clear, in order to be considered polite, sociable, mature, intelligent, and so on, it is essential to know when to criticize the state as non-democratic and when to keep quiet.[38] It may be fine to express a dissatisfaction with democratic institutions during seminar, among friends, or when excused as a joke, but not when discussing political preferences, standing in line to vote, or otherwise engaging in activities that presuppose the possibility of popular sovereignty. To answer the questions "Who are you voting for?" or "What is your position?" by pointing out that it hardly matters is not only considered ill-mannered and inappropriate, but often naive or irresponsible as well, evoking a knee-jerk defense of democratic institutions that, upon further reflection and under less confrontational circumstances, may itself prove unfounded. To regularly or categorically highlight democracy's failure is to expose that kernel, one otherwise submerged beneath layers of history, identity, tradition, habits, and niceties, and force a confrontation with what many would rather be left unsaid, often provoking responses that range from an unpleasant awkwardness to outright hostility. In this way, it is like dredging up another's faults or other private matters considered rude to discuss in public. This is not to suggest that all citizens are at all times carrying with them some secret democratic guilt, anxious to confront it. Most remain unaware, either disinterested in politics or further examining their relationship to it. For those who are aware, it is a problem they can do little about, and most prefer not to dwell on it.

32 What is Post-Democracy?

Beyond offering an escape from the dreary reality of a non-democratic present, people tend to enjoy the fantasy of democratic citizenship. They like discussing politics as if their opinions carried political force, reading about politics in order to stay informed, imagining themselves as fulfilling some sacred, civic duty, and voting with the belief that they influence policymaking. Politics can be fun: the rallies, the protests, and the marches, not to mention the bumper stickers, T-shirts, buttons, and other ephemera. Additionally, many consider their political beliefs to be an existentially significant aspect of their character, making the encouraged opportunity to express them something difficult to dismiss. All of this helps to sustain a social reality that not only distracts from the awful, open secret of democratic failure, but is pleasurable in itself, a way of feeling empowered and seeing the state as an extension of the citizenry. This last point is especially important when asked to make sacrifices for the state. Whether paying taxes, following the law, or going to war, individuals want to believe that they have some say in the matter, making their decision to obey an instance of autonomy rather than deference. Overall, thinking of oneself as a democratic citizen feels better, and in a society that insists on treating people as such, it ultimately seems easier as well.

At the heart of the post-democratic experience, then, is the paradoxical, yet inescapable perception that one both is and is not a democratic citizen.[39] On the one hand, to recognize post-democracy is to know that democratic institutions are failing or have failed and acknowledge, at least on a theoretical level, that democratic citizenship is collapsing or has already collapsed. In some intellectual and political circles, this position is hardly novel, thus making it possible to live an authentically post-democratic life in which one scoffs at all forms of mass political participation and talks about the state as if it were some criminal organization. But few live their entire lives in such circles, and even those who do are never completely insulated from a broader, democratic political culture that continues to address them, as it has ever since they were young, *as if* they were democratic citizens. Thus, most remain wrapped up in a persistently and overtly democratic social reality that continues to largely determine the substance and limits of their political existence.

This is what makes the term "post-democracy" so uniquely apropos. It names a context that, despite not truly being democratic, remains so wedded to the concept that it could not be anything but democratic, making it impossible to describe it as anything else. To simply default to oligarchy or authoritarianism is to miss the pervasive and hegemonic role played by the ongoing belief in democracy and democratic institutions, as well as the persistent temptation to indulge in the fantasy of democratic citizenship. Certainly, post-democracies have explicit oligarchic or authoritarian tendencies, but the collective, prevailing assumption is still that something like democracy exists, or that it did and can again, ruling out those tendencies as anomalous. It is thus not conceptually or experientially oligarchic or authoritarian, even if it is practically so, because it does

What is Post-Democracy? **33**

not adequately express the peculiarity of feeling both empowered and powerless; significant and negligible; hopeful and resigned; autonomous and dominated. Only post-democracy articulates the ubiquity of democratic thinking and the weight of democratic inheritance alongside the political inequality and persistent frustration that define the ordinary experience of contemporary political life.

The Problem of Post-Democracy

The central problem of post-democratic theory, then, is reconciling the failure of democratic institutions and subsequent loss of democratic citizenship with an enduring democratic cultural horizon; in other words, how to move beyond the ideological fantasy of democratic citizenship to a more honest engagement with the broader implications of post-democratic sovereignty. For many, this may be a problem not worth addressing. As noted above, people enjoy acting like a democratic citizen, even when they know better, seeming to make the system sustainable to the extent it offers electoral turnover (even if between two elite-dominated, fairly similar parties), giving voters the opportunity to confuse their candidate's victory with evidence of popular sovereignty or political equality. For some, however, this is not enough, and the need for a more sustained investigation into both the post-democratic state and their relationship to it outweighs the comforts of an unexamined life. A general theory of post-democracy is intended to facilitate that investigation.

In order to illustrate what is at stake in the problem, it is essential to consider how a greater awareness of political powerlessness would necessarily affect the theoretical assumptions that underpin a democratic conception of citizenship. Generally, democratic theory understands the citizen as a political decision-maker. Even models of democracy which do not rely on widespread, active participation still require citizens to occasionally make meaningful decisions (e.g., which representative to elect, whether the public discourse lives up to deliberative ideals). This role then informs the citizen's relationship to both the state and other citizens. A political system is legitimate to the extent that ordinary citizens play a significant role in the decision-making process. Citizens consider themselves members of their political community by virtue of their ability to participate in that decision-making process. Subsequently, citizens feel as if they have some responsibility to the state (e.g., a *prima facie* reason for following the law or volunteering for service), as well as the sense that they should bear some guilt for the 'crimes' of their political community. These transgressions may be excused by necessity (e.g., imminent domain, collateral damage), but some may be inexcusable (e.g., massacres, genocides). All the same, to govern (or even to freely choose those who will) invites this burden.

When ordinary citizens are unable to see themselves as decision-makers, this logic no longer suffices. Take the question of political legitimacy. Unable to democratically legitimate the state, the post-democratic citizen is left to either

34 What is Post-Democracy?

find new legitimating criteria or consider the possibility of being governed by an illegitimate sovereign power. For those pursuing the first option, liberalism is the most likely substitute. In exchange for the freedom of both speech and contract and the rights to property and due process, a fair number of individuals would probably be fine with giving up on the hope of exercising political influence. Yet, this must be a liberalism that does not rely on any sort of democratic guarantee or remedy; a liberalism, *contra* Judith Shklar's liberalism of fear, divorced from democracy.[40] There are undoubtedly other mechanisms for promoting a liberal polity, whether through the efforts of a virtuous aristocracy, benevolent despot, or philosopher king, or, as is increasingly evident, a *modus vivendi* between oligarchs, that may actually prove more effective than democracy at maintaining liberal norms. Still, post-democracy's propensity for spectacle, demagogues, and the politicization of private life may just as quickly turn to threaten liberal norms; clearly, it already has.

There are, of course, other criteria one could use to legitimate the post-democratic state. Some more popular options might include a Hobbesian cessation of violence, a paternalistic consideration of a population's well-being (e.g., the enforcement of health codes, environmental and consumer protections), or an ability to foster economic prosperity. Two somewhat less contingent measures include identifying with the state based upon certain existential criteria (e.g., one's ethnicity, religion, or, circularly, one's nationality) or the intrinsic authority of the state's founders or its sacred texts, though divorced from any democratic interpretation. In any case, choosing a substitute for democracy puts the individual at odds with the prevailing democratic political imaginary inherent in post-democracy, still necessitating a deeper engagement with how that substitute unsettles the possibility for sincere participation in a democratic social reality. In other words, it means admitting that state legitimacy no longer depends upon the ability to govern oneself; that it is not a matter of choosing, but of accepting the choices made by others.[41]

The other possibility, of course, is to recognize the state as lacking any claim to legitimacy at all. Just because the criteria of popular sovereignty and political equality are not satisfied does not mean that one must give up on them. Yet, this means having to seriously wrestle with the idea that the state's use of violence may be morally indistinguishable from unjust or criminal acts. While perhaps easy to imagine, this process may be more difficult than one realizes at first. For example, it may be possible to shrug off a speeding ticket with an easy dismissal or sort of noblesse oblige, but it seems more difficult to do so after being subject to property seizure, harassment by law enforcement, incarceration, or the loss of a loved one at the hands of the state. And while some may occasionally make the Thoreauvian gesture of defiance, not all can afford it. After all, even Thoreau regularly paid his taxes.

Similarly, a lack of political power disturbs democratic assumptions about their membership in a political community. A post-democratic diagnosis would mean that a vast majority of citizens are excluded from any sort of political community, properly understood. Unable to exercise any sort of significant political influence, they can at best imagine themselves as part of a national community, largely, if not exclusively, based on their status as legal subjects. For many, this may be enough. Yet, it is important to remember that, without the possibility for democratic political action, their membership in a national community would be purely passive. They would not constitute a 'we,' but merely an 'us,' united solely by the shared experience of being governed. This may further give the impression that one's membership in a national community is ultimately insignificant. Unable to look to neighbors as partners in a collective political project, an individual may begin to feel detached from them, at least in the sense of having any kind of shared political destiny. In this sense, post-democracy illuminates the political isolation of the governed. This feeling is only exacerbated by the awareness of continuing to be surrounded by self-understood democratic citizens. In addition to the general feeling of political powerlessness, the post-democratic citizens remain trapped in a larger political culture unwilling to consider the greater consequences of their predicament. Like Nietzsche's madman, surrounded by those who do not yet realize what it means now that God is dead, they will necessarily feel a kind of epistemic alienation, as if living in a different reality from those around them.[42]

Citizens must also grapple with their sense of responsibility to the state—in particular, whether they ought to follow the law or volunteer for service—as well as any feelings of culpability for its transgressions. Both would largely depend upon one's conception of legitimacy, though not entirely. One might not consider the state legitimate, but still avoid breaking the law or dodging military service in order to escape punishment or protect the safety of one's family. This does not seem to suggest a direct responsibility to the state as much as a responsibility to oneself and others that can best be realized by acting in accordance with the state's wishes. In contrast, citizens might feel absolved of any responsibility to the state, feeling justified not only in avoiding all forms of service but even in breaking the law, assuming it furthers their interests and does not put them at significant risk of being punished. Thus, citizens might feel comfortable cheating on their taxes, defrauding state institutions, or committing perjury. Moral obligations may keep them from indiscriminately raping and pillaging, but they lack any sort of political obligation that would keep them from taking advantage of the state or one another.

The question of culpability, however, is harder to resolve; citizens may decide to disregard their alleged political responsibilities, but it is much more difficult to shrug off the sense that they lack any responsibility for the crimes committed in their name.[43] A persistent, pervasive democratic rhetoric can make citizens feel as if they are nevertheless to blame for all of the destructive policy decisions, military incursions, and instances of police misconduct in which they played no part. Even lacking all political power, citizens may feel as if they let these crimes happen and, as such, must either atone or find some way of proving to themselves and others

36 What is Post-Democracy?

that they did all in their power to prevent it. The post-war critique of 'ordinary Germans' has left many with the sense that people are always to blame for their government's actions, but it also leads some to forget that serious efforts to confront the state, even during better times, are rarely more than symbolic. As it is for each of the other considerations, whether a deeper feeling of culpability is either productive or escapable will ultimately be specific to each individual.

While hardly exhaustive, this basic framework of considerations—legitimacy, membership, responsibility, and culpability—gives us a way of thinking about some of the more immediate theoretical concerns resulting from a post-democratic diagnosis. How, then, can we begin to address these urgent questions and develop a thoroughly post-democratic theory of politics? The next chapter explores three possible approaches: democratic realism, democratic idealism, and post-democratic acknowledgment; ultimately arguing for the latter and a sustained examination of the theoretical implications of a persistently post-democratic existence.

Notes

1   Rancière [1992] 1995, p. 35, Rancière [1995] 1999, p. 95
2   Wolin 2001, ch. 26
3   Crouch 2000, Crouch 2004
4   Rorty 2004. For more on Rorty's decision to title the piece, see Postel 2007.
5   Fonte 2004
6   For instance, see Baumier 2007, Béal 2011, Blühdorn 2014, Glassman 2007, Glassman 2010, and Laffin 2016.
7   Habermas 2012. See also Katsambekis 2017.
8   This workshop led to a series of short papers by Andre Willis, Eduardo Mendieta, James Martel, and Marc Stears, all found in *Juncture* (2015) 22(3): 201–219.
9   Rancière [1995] 1999, pp. 100–103
10 Rancière [1995] 1999, pp. 102–108. Cf. Arendt [1963] 2006, ch. 6
11 Crouch 2004, p. 21
12 Wolin 2001, p. 571
13 Crouch 2004, p. 21
14 Fonte 2004; Habermas 2012, p. 48, *italics in original*
15 Rorty 2004
16 Crouch 2004, p. 22
17 Ercan and Gagnon 2014, pp. 5–6
18 Thucydides 1972, p. 145
19 This is not to suggest that the question of 'who' constitutes the People is ever truly settled. Obviously, we continue to debate about the status of felons, undocumented immigrants, even children. However, those debates are also recognized as open; it is one thing to suggest that a felon not be able to vote, but another to argue that women, minorities, or the poor be barred from politics (even if being a member of a minority community or poor makes you systematically more likely to become a felon). On some level, it is a matter of semantics, but semantics still play a decisive role concerning specifically which forms of disenfranchisement are acceptable and which are not.
20 Schumpeter [1942] 1954, pp. 284–285
21 Green 2016, ch. 2
22 Bodin [1606] 1962, p. 84

23 Hobbes [1668] 1994, XVII.4
24 Weber [1946] 2004, p. 33
25 Schmitt [1932] 2007, p. 33
26 Schmitt [1932] 2007, pp. 47–48; Weber [1946] 2004, p. 33
27 See, for instance, the recent literature on 'engaged citizenship,' including Inglehart 1997, Zukin et al. 2006, Bennett 2008, and Dalton 2008a and 2008b.
28 See Rancière [1995] 1999, Zizek [1999] 2008, and Mouffe 2005.
29 Welch 2013
30 Crouch 2015, pp. 73–74
31 See Mouffe 2005, pp. 45–51.
32 Crouch 2004, p. 7
33 Martel 2015, p. 210
34 They may, in fact, be helping people, but post-democracy implies a series of enduring, structural obstacles that fundamentally limit the ability of political leaders to do anything more than imitate popular sovereignty.
35 Rancière [1995] 1999, p. 101
36 Zizek 1989, p. 45
37 Zizek 1989, p. 36
38 Zizek 2010, pp. 4–9
39 Rancière similarly describes post-democracy as paradoxical, but in the sense that a fictional "People," fabricated by public opinion polls and electoral results, come to rule in place of real citizens (Rancière [1995] 1999, p. 101).
40 See Shklar 1998.
41 The one exception would be those who do still influence political decision-making; they may still legitimate the state based upon their own participation, but not upon the idea of collective participation.
42 Nietzsche [1882] 1974, pp. 181–182
43 See Beerbohm 2012.

References

Arendt, Hannah. *On Revolution*. Chicago: University of Chicago Press, [1963] 2006.
Baumier, Matthieu. *La démocratie totalitaire: Penser la modernité post-démocratique*. Paris: Presses de la Renaissance, 2007.
Béal, Vincent. "Urban Governance, Sustainability and Environmental Movements: Post-Democracy in French and British Cities," *European Urban and Regional Studies* 19. 4 (December 2011): 404–419.
Beerbohm, Eric. *In Our Names: The Ethics of Democracy*. Princeton, NJ: Princeton UP, 2012.
Bennett, W. Lance. "Civic Learning in Changing Democracies: Challenges for Citizenship and Civic Education" in *Young Citizens and New Media: Learning and Democratic Engagement*. Peter Dahlgren, ed. New York: Routledge, 2008.
Blühdorn, Ingolfur. "Post-Ecologist Governmentality: Post-Democracy, Post-Politics and the Politics of Unsustainability," in *The Post-Political and its Discontents: Spaces of Depoliticisation, Spectres of Radical Politics*. Erik Swyngedouw and Japhy Wilson, eds. Edinburgh: Edinburgh UP, 2014: 146–166.
Bodin, Jean. *The Six Books of a Commonweale*. Cambridge, MA: Harvard UP, [1606] 1962.
Crouch, Colin. *Coping with Post-Democracy*. London: Fabian Society, 2000.
Crouch, Colin. *Post-Democracy*. Malden, MA: Polity Press, 2004.
Crouch, Colin. *The Knowledge Corrupters: Hidden Consequences of the Financial Takeover of Public Life*. Malden, MA: Polity Press, 2015.

38 What is Post-Democracy?

Dalton, Russell J. "Citizenship Norms and the Expansion of Political Participation," *Political Studies* 56. 1 (March 2008a): 76–98.

Dalton, Russel J. *The Good Citizen: How a Younger Generation is Reshaping American Politics.* Washington, D.C.: CQ Press, 2008b.

Ercan, Selen A. and Jean-Paul Gagnon. "The Crisis of Democracy: Which Crisis? Which Democracy?" *Democratic Theory* 1. 2 (Winter 2014): 1–10.

Fonte, John. "Democracy's Trojan Horse," *The National Interest* (June 2004). Web. <https://nationalinterest.org/article/democracys-trojan-horse-1155>. Accessed July 20, 2019.

Glassman, Jim. "Post-Democracy?" *Environment and Planning A: Economy and Space* 39. 9 (September 2007): 2037–2042.

Glassman, Jim. "'The Provinces Elect Governments, Bangkok Overthrows Them': Urbanity, Class, and Post-Democracy in Thailand," *Urban Studies* 47. 6 (May 2010): 1301–1323.

Green, Jeffrey Edward. *The Shadow of Unfairness: A Plebeian Theory of Liberal Democracy.* New York: Oxford UP, 2016.

Habermas, Jurgen. *The Crisis of the European Union: A Response.* Malden, MA: Polity Press, 2012.

Hobbes, Thomas. *Leviathan.* Indianapolis, IN: Hackett Publishing, [1668] 1994.

Katsambekis, Giorgos. "The Populist Surge in Post-Democratic Times: Theoretical and Political Challenges," *The Political Quarterly* 88. 2 (April–June 2017): 202–210.

Inglehart, Ronald. *Modernization and Postmodernization: Cultural, Economic, and Political Change in 43 Societies.* Princeton, NJ: Princeton UP, 1997.

Laffin, Martin. "Planning in England: New Public Management, Network Governance or Post-Democracy?" *International Review of Administrative Sciences* 82. 2 (June 2016): 354–372.

Martel, James. "Are We 'Post-Democratic'—Or Have We Not (Yet) Been Democratic At All?" *Juncture* 22. 3 (Winter 2015): 210–215.

Mouffe, Chantal. *On the Political.* New York: Routledge, 2005.

Nietzsche, Friedrich. *The Gay Science: With a Prelude in Rhymes and an Appendix of Songs.* New York: Vintage Books, [1882] 1974.

Postel, Danny. "Last Words from Richard Rorty," *The Progressive* (June 11, 2007). Web. <https://progressive.org/magazine/last-words-richard-rorty/>. Accessed July 20, 2019.

Rancière, Jacques. *On the Shores of Politics.* New York: Verso Press, [1992] 1995.

Rancière, Jacques. *Dis-agreement: Politics and Philosophy.* Minneapolis, MN: University of Minnesota Press, [1995] 1999.

Rorty, Richard. "Post-Democracy: Richard Rorty on Anti-Terrorism and the National Security State," *London Review of Books* 26. 7 (April 1, 2004): 10–11.

Schmitt, Carl. *The Concept of the Political.* Chicago: University of Chicago Press, [1932] 2007.

Schumpeter, Joseph. *Capitalism, Socialism, and Democracy.* New York: Ruskin House, [1942] 1954.

Shklar, Judith. "The Liberalism of Fear" in *Political Thought and Political Thinkers.* Stanley Hoffmann, ed. Chicago: University of Chicago Press, 1998.

Thucydides. *History of the Peloponnesian War.* Trans: Rex Warner. New York: Penguin Classics, 1972.

Weber, Max. "Politics as Vocation" in *The Vocation Lectures.* Indianapolis, IN: Hackett Publishing, [1946] 2004.

Welch, Stephen. *Hyperdemocracy.* New York: Palgrave Macmillan, 2013.

Wolin, Sheldon S. *Tocqueville Between Two Worlds: The Making of a Political and Theoretical Life.* Princeton, NJ: Princeton UP, 2001.

Zizek, Slavoj. *The Sublime Object of Ideology*. New York: Verso Press, 1989.

Zizek, Slavoj. *The Ticklish Subject: The Absent Centre of Political Ontology*. New York: Verso Press, [1999] 2008.

Zizek, Slavoj. *Living in the End Times*. New York: Verso Press, 2010.

Zukin, Cliff, Scott Keeter, Molly Andolina, Krista Jenkins, and Michael X. Delli Carpini. *A New Engagement? Political Participation, Civil Life, and the Changing American Citizen*. New York: Oxford UP, 2006.

3

IDEALISM, REALISM, AND ACKNOWLEDGMENT

The central problem of post-democratic theory is the problem of political powerlessness: how should self-understood democratic citizens respond to their lack of popular sovereignty or political equality? In this chapter, we explore three possible approaches for addressing this problem. The first, democratic idealism, seeks to overturn or undo non-democratic conditions, treating post-democracy as a practical problem. The second, democratic realism, critiques the expectation of either popular sovereignty or political equality, characterizing post-democracy as the result of a conceptual misunderstanding, one that can be dispelled by adopting a more chastened, procedural interpretation of democracy. Together, these two approaches are broadly representative of the state of democratic theory, as well as the ways in which post-democratic theorists themselves have begun to tackle the problem thus far.

While illuminating in their own ways, both approaches ultimately prove inadequate for engaging with either the enduring conceptual or normative implications of mass political powerlessness. On the one hand, democratic idealists tend to focus exclusively on strategy, that is, developing new and better models of democratic practice and citizenship. In doing so, they ignore the more immediate consequences of post-democracy: the unavoidable implications of this powerlessness for how citizens think about their relationship to the state, each other, and themselves. On the other hand, despite encouraging citizens to recognize the more sobering features of mass politics—a largely inactive public, *de facto* elite rule—democratic realists underestimate citizens' sincere, collective attachment to democratic values, too easily dismissing this attachment in favor of the *mere appearance* of popular sovereignty or political equality. Thus, realists end up missing the far-reaching, normative implications of democracy's absence, the anxieties and frustrations that continue to animate democratic idealists, such as whether elite domination makes a democratic state illegitimate, whether it is wrong to tolerate an illegitimate state, or whether the failure to become a democratic citizen constitutes a moral or ethical failing.

Thinking through the often distressing theoretical and normative repercussions of political powerlessness requires a different sort of approach, one that does not treat powerlessness as a problem to be solved, but as a persistent feature of mass democratic politics. In short, the problem of post-democracy requires a distinctly post-democratic perspective. After a brief survey of both of the predominant approaches, this chapter will introduce a third approach, one which does not avoid or downplay the consequences of a post-democratic diagnosis for citizens' political self-understanding, but confronts them directly by acknowledging mass political powerlessness as a brute fact of post-democratic life. This acknowledgment has significant implications not only for how citizens understand themselves—their beliefs about legitimacy, membership, responsibility, and culpability now available to them—but for the very tools they use to do so: the reading and writing of political philosophy and mass participation (e.g., voting, protest, discussion). Previously, these tools were oriented toward the exercise of political power; changing the world, as Marx said, rather than merely interpreting it. Under post-democracy, they must be repurposed. To understand why such a radical shift is necessary, we must first explore the ways in which our present alternatives fail to meet the challenges of the present.

Democratic Idealism

For many, the obvious response to the problem of political powerlessness will be a call to fix it, to restore or realize some degree of popular sovereignty and political equality. Those who make this call are democratic idealists. The use of the term idealist should not be understood as conveying any sort of inherent utopianism or naiveté, but simply to reflect the aspirational quality of the effort. In fact, democratic idealists are typically those with the least naiveté when it comes to political matters. They clearly recognize the current obstacles to democratic practice and endeavor to publicize and overcome them. As Sidney Hook said of life itself, politics as a whole is a tragic business, a fraught, difficult, demanding activity, which regularly produces winners and losers under less-than-fair conditions, and even if things can be improved, this would not change the challenges intrinsic to it.[1] Fully aware of these conditions, democratic idealists refuse to submit, maintaining that any alternative to democracy or democratic thinking is simply unacceptable. In this sense, they remain both conceptually committed to democratic theory and, for the most part, resolute in their optimism for a democratic future.

Most of contemporary political theory can be found in this camp; they may disagree about the proper definition or interpretation of democracy, but they agree that the People should, can, and, hopefully will have a meaningful voice in

42 Idealism, Realism, and Acknowledgment

political decision-making. This category includes all those interested in elaborating or promoting new or better ways of thinking about mass participation, representation, civic virtue, deliberation, the range and nature of political conflict, forms of citizenship, and so on, always with the aim of politically empowering ordinary citizens.[2] From this perspective, post-democracy is certainly a problem, but one citizens must respond to through political action. The position is perhaps best captured in the findings of that first North American workshop on post-democracy briefly mentioned in the previous chapter, which Andre Willis summarizes as follows: "if the concept of post-democracy could be of any use then it would have to expand democratic possibilities from below and shore up democratic institutions from above, while working towards more socioeconomic equality."[3] In other words, if post-democracy is to have any import at all, it must provide some sort of practical import for democratic activism and reform.

For Crouch, Habermas, and Rorty, this certainly seems to be the case. Crouch uses the term to highlight the political consequences of neoliberalism; Habermas, the absence of a distinctly European political consciousness; and Rorty, the increasing securitization of liberal democracies. In effect, each uses the term to draw attention to a set of problems which require citizens' attention, problems they hope can be solved before they become much worse. For instance, Rorty calls upon citizens to "challenge the culture of government secrecy," specifically "in the areas of nuclear weaponry and intelligence-gathering," as well as to "demand that their governments join efforts to update the laws of war, and to create something like a code of international criminal justice."[4] Habermas emphasizes that "the more that national populations realize ... how profoundly the decisions of the European Union pervade their daily lives, the more their interest in making use of their democratic rights also as EU citizens will increase," further calling on European elites to cultivate a shared European political consciousness through "a risky, and above all inspired, struggle within the broad public."[5]

Crouch offers by far the most comprehensive approach to post-democracy. Focusing on the need to prevent global business interests from further dominating the political process, he concerns himself mainly with the problems that stem from a corrupted party system. While still the best organ for popular politics, these parties remain dominated by elite interests. As Crouch points out, "governmental and party policy-making machinery, even of left-of-centre parties, has itself become endogenous to the problem of the power of the corporate elite."[6] To confront this problem, Crouch argues for embracing more egalitarian political practices (e.g., citizens' assemblies), fostering government services and mass participation on a local level, and working "critically and conditionally" with major political parties, while also trying to exert popular pressure on those parties through cause organizations and social movements, at times by even threatening to withhold support.[7] In this way, citizens can force parties to pursue egalitarian interests they otherwise would

Idealism, Realism, and Acknowledgment **43**

not, enabling them some means of contesting the political influence exercised by corporate and other elite interests.[8] This requires being attentive to new movements and political identities, which Crouch describes as "the seedbeds of future democratic vitality," noting that "democratic politics ... needs a vigorous, chaotic, noisy context of movements and groups."[9]

As Crouch points out, however, this support for independent groups, especially as a means for directing mass parties, effectively replicates the elite lobbying tactics that weakened the mass party in the first place and, thus, democracy as a whole, paradoxically, further contributing to post-democratic conditions. He summarizes the problem in writing,

> On the one hand, it would seem that in post-democratic society we can no longer take for granted the commitment of particular parties to particular causes. This would lead to the conclusion that we should turn our backs on the party fight and devote our energies to cause organizations ... On the other hand we have also seen that the fragmentation of political action into a mass of causes and lobbies provides systematic advantages to the rich.[10]

Ultimately, Crouch advises engaging in professional lobbying all the same, recognizing that "even if the causes supported by egalitarians are always weaker there than those of the large corporation, they are weaker still if they stay out of the lobby."[11] Citizens must 'play the game,' as it were, if they are to have any hope of affecting the outcomes.

Yet, the major objection to Crouch's position is not that an active citizenry could inadvertently further a post-democratic politics of interest group lobbying; to the extent that citizens are able to achieve egalitarian reforms, such tactics would seem worth the risks posed to an otherwise inegalitarian system. Rather, the real concern is where we might expect to find such an active citizenry in the first place. Crouch stresses from the beginning that post-democracy is marked precisely by political inactivity on the part of ordinary people.[12] To assume citizens capable of such coordinated action as to be able to hold mass parties accountable is to hastily dismiss the very problem of post-democracy itself, calling upon an organized, empowered citizenry to make up for the absence of an organized, empowered citizenry.

To his credit, Couch acknowledges the inherent challenges facing any sort of popular strategy against post-democracy, recognizing that the democratic distortions of the present "are so powerful and widespread that it is impossible to see any major reversal of them."[13] What he suggests, he does so in faith that some "actions to try to shift contemporary politics partly away from the inexorable drift towards post-democracy are possible."[14] Habermas exhibits a similar sort of skepticism in his own proposal, pointing out that a European political consciousness would "paradoxically" require that elites

44 Idealism, Realism, and Acknowledgment

> Would have to strive for something in the common European weal that runs counter to their own interest in maintaining power. For, in the long run, the scope of action at the national level would become narrower and the importance of the appearance of national potentates on the political stage would diminish.[15]

Rather, when looking to Brexit and the broader Eurosceptic movement, it seems much more likely that many elites will continue to exploit feelings of antipathy toward the EU for their own political and economic advantage, shunning the greater prospect of a genuinely democratic Europe to line their own pockets and further entrench their interests. Those elites who do support a united Europe may be just as interested in the sort of economic and political benefits they could reap from the common market and a steady hand in Brussels as they are in making Europe more democratic, assuming the latter interests them at all. This is to say nothing of the other obstacle Habermas identifies—economic disparity—which his book on the European Union leaves unaddressed.[16] Rorty, however, remains the most cynical of all, imagining that in,

> A worst-case scenario, historians will someday have to explain why the golden age of Western democracy ... lasted only about two hundred years. The saddest pages in their books are likely to be those in which they describe how the citizens of the democracies, by their craven acquiescence in governmental secrecy, helped bring the disaster on themselves.[17]

This deep-seated pessimism marks all three works and, while warranted, undercuts the force of their prescriptions, transforming what would be, under more democratic conditions, reasonable or realistic proposals for reform into desperate, if not resigned pleas for salvation. Ultimately, unable to facilitate any further engagement with the enduring conditions of political powerlessness, these proposals do little more for ordinary citizens than remind them of what has been lost. In short, they offer no way forward.

Overall, Crouch, Rorty, and Habermas all remain committed to democratic thinking in a way that prevents a more exhaustive account of post-democratic politics. According to the idealist perspective, elite domination—in all its myriad forms—is something to be overcome, not to be fleshed out; and yet, this leaves citizens woefully unprepared to confront a political context in which that domination may just as likely continue, if not get worse. This fidelity to democratic ideals, to the point of refusing to consider any alternative, is admirable, but ultimately inadequate to the task at hand, which requires not simply a criticism of post-democratic conditions, but an appropriate way of responding to them, one which attends to the problem of powerlessness as more than a complication or setback, but as an enduring condition of mass politics.

Inexorable Idealism

Still, it could be argued that the issue with Crouch, Rorty, and Habermas's response to post-democracy is not their (lapsing) commitment to a democratic future, but the way in which they understand the nature of democratic practice itself. Specifically, in despairing over the possibility of a satisfactorily democratic state, they miss the intrinsically agonistic character of democracy, one in which conflict, often between asymmetrical parties, is always unfolding. From this perspective, popular sovereignty and political equality are not given, but ever-evolving projects, the result of persistent democratic struggle. In fact, as Bonnie Honig persuasively argues in her book, *Democracy and the Foreigner*, perspectives like Rorty's, which insist on the citizen's "total identification" with the state, contribute to the very "paralyzing paranoia" on the Left Rorty otherwise decries, if not further encouraging citizens to adopt a simplistic 'us vs. them' political mentality.[18] Rather, Honig suggests that citizens "nurture some ambivalence regarding their principles, their leaders, and their neighbors …[and] to be wary of authorities and powers that seek to govern us, claiming to know what is in our best interests."[19] Such an ambivalence would treat the various causes of post-democracy as problems, but post-democracy itself as one more manifestation of the "paralyzing paranoia" that only advances a general "spirit of detached spectatorship" in politics.[20]

Based on her masterfully inventive reading of gothic romance novels like Daphne du Maurier's *Rebecca* and Charlotte Bronte's *Jane Eyre*, Honig instead proposes a seasoned, suspicious, *gothic* model of democratic subjectivity, one which stresses that

> the subjects best prepared for the demands of democracy are those who exist in agonistic relation to a founder (or a father or law) whose alienness is a poorly kept secret; subjects who do not expect power to be granted to them by nice authorities … with their best interests at heart … subjects who know that if they want power they must take it … subjects who know that such takings are always illegitimate from the perspective of the order in place at the time … subjects who know that their efforts to carve out a just and legitimate polity will always be haunted by the violence of their founding … subjects who experience the law … as a horizon of promise, but also as an alien and impositional thing.[21]

These are citizens who will not be deterred by less-than-ideal democratic conditions, such as they are; if politics was already fair and just, they tell us, it would not be politics. In fostering this sort of oppositional relationship to both the state and other citizens, the gothic subject appears ready not only to challenge the conditions of post-democracy, but to thrive in them.

This position again assumes, however, a particularly involved citizenry; citizens can hardly be described as being in an "agonistic relation" to the state, 'taking

46 Idealism, Realism, and Acknowledgment

power' and 'carving out a just and legitimate polity,' unless actively engaged in at least some domain of political struggle. Otherwise, the issue would not be becoming comfortable with a certain degree of ambivalence in politics, but finding a way into politics at all. This entrance would perhaps be indistinguishable from the business of politics itself, and would undoubtedly benefit from the sort of virtues and dispositions Honig praises, but still depends, in the last instance, on both the citizen's willingness to participate and their ability to do so in a sustained, deliberate manner. Under post-democratic conditions, neither should so readily be assumed. Of course, there are those who ignore politics all together, but there are also those who, while not exactly apathetic, are not quite participants either; those who read and discuss politics, but are too busy or too burdened to do more than vote, perhaps even limiting themselves only to major elections. Some know they should be doing more, while others imagine that they are already doing enough; in either case, they seem to fall far below the level of political engagement at which Honig's gothic disposition becomes relevant.

Of those who do regularly participate, involved in this or that effort, there seems to be the further expectation that these citizens, if only occasionally, find some success, making the law not simply "an alien and impositional thing," but also "a horizon of promise." In other words, even if citizens do not totally identify with the state, they should, from time to time, be able to recognize their imprint on it. Under post-democratic conditions, this, too, may be too much to assume. Post-democracy names a context not simply in which political institutions are unbalanced, but either dominated, corrupt, or otherwise hollow; as such, the state is not a site of democratic contestation, but itself, at least as far as ordinary citizens are concerned, a truly 'alien' institution. As such, rather than simply feeling ambivalent about the state, post-democratic actors may be better served by an attitude of estrangement.

And yet, there are those who would respond that nothing—not even (or perhaps especially) recognizing the estrangement of the state or one's own community—should dissuade citizens from their commitment to democratic values and, subsequently, their efforts to protect or restore a democratic way of life. This commitment is perhaps best captured by Aletta Norval's compelling figuration of democracy as a promise.[22] In her powerful book, *Aversive Democracy*, Norval describes herself as responding to "an inevitable sense of 'restiveness,'" she finds in contemporary politics, "which is often expressed in terms of disappointment with the ongoing practices associated with contemporary democratic life, driven as it is by a sense that things could be better."[23] Building on a Cavellian-infused reading of Jacques Derrida's 'democracy to come,' she argues that democracy cannot be reduced to a set of institutional arrangements, but instead represents a promise to pursue democratic community, "a promise that is kept in memory, that is handed down ... inherited, claimed, taken up," a project with which citizens will never be satisfied and, thus, an infinite call to become better versions of themselves.[24] When considering contemporary obstacles to democracy, this view encourages citizens to recognize themselves as part of a long tradition of democratic struggle, one which requires them to adopt certain democratic dispositions (e.g., critical thinking, attending to one's community, taking responsibility for it) in order to maintain this promise of democratic citizenship. She herself writes of South Africa's Truth and Reconciliation Commission, the nation's efforts to explore and overcome the abuses and horrors of Apartheid, as a striking example of democratic responsiveness and community building, one which empowered a new, self-aware citizenry to emerge.[25]

This sort of position certainly seems right, resonating with the feeling of infinite debt cultivated by democratic tradition and culture. For committed democratic citizens, it provides reassurance that their efforts are not in vain, but part of a larger, historical project, in turn, inspiring continued democratic participation and activism. Moreover, examples like that of South African Apartheid highlight the way in which democratic reform—whether institutional, civic, discursive, and so on—is not only possible, but achievable, even under the worst of circumstances. When contrasted with such examples, the idea that the present impediments to popular sovereignty are insurmountable seems silly, even offensive; rather, the only real issue becomes the apparent unwillingness on the part of ordinary citizens to rise to the occasion and become the sort of democratic citizens they otherwise aspire to be.

And yet, post-democracy results from precisely the sort of mass political apathy and conformism Norval warns us against. Instead of taking up the mantle of democratic citizenship, educating and informing themselves, getting involved in public life, enforcing deliberative norms, and so on, ordinary citizens may just as well continue to prioritize their immediate self-interests at the expense of their community's collective concerns. Or, and perhaps worse, citizens will increasingly get involved in politics in decidedly non-democratic fashions, dismissing Norval's democratic perfectionism (or, for that matter, any form of democratic subjectivity) in favor of Augustinian authoritarianism, Nietzschean elitism, or *Blut und Boden*-style populism.[26] In either case, regardless of any individual commitment to a democracy-to-come, the kind of democratic contestation Honig and Norval celebrate would cease to play a major role in public life. And while history is nothing if not surprising, it is also often predictable—at times, even frighteningly so—suggesting that we have just as much (if not more) reason to fear further democratic malaise as we do to look forward to a brighter future or even, for that matter, a tolerable one.

For Norval, ordinary citizens should be willing to weather this sort of cynicism; democracy depends on it. But at what point is disappointment warranted? Or, rather, at what point should ongoing or increasing disappointments justify skepticism or even suspicion towards democratic possibility in the present? Regardless of their attachment to democratic values, at what point should citizens acknowledge that they no longer live in a democracy, that they live an insufficiently democratic way of life and will, most likely, continue to do so? And, moreover, when should this awareness begin to affect how citizens imagine their relationship to politics, the state, and one another?

48 Idealism, Realism, and Acknowledgment

For the idealist, this line of thought is, at best, a distraction; at worst, it is counterproductive and defeatist. However, for those either less resolute, more pessimistic, or simply more flexible, post-democratic conditions require us to move beyond traditional democratic concepts and categories and, above all, the base assumption that ordinary citizens can or will participate in politics in a deliberate or undistorted manner. Of course, there will always be individual exceptions—the veneer of democracy would be impossible without it—but, at present, they continue to be just that, exceptions, and not at all indicative of day-to-day politics. Thus, we should not confuse the two. To do so risks sustaining, if not further inspiring, an ideological fantasy of democratic citizenship, one that both mystifies the People's present role in mass democracy and perhaps even bestows a false sense of confidence or satisfaction, especially among those less gothic or aversive than Honig or Norval would like or imagine them to be. Rather, a deeper engagement with post-democracy requires us to explore the banal, yet disheartening implications of a demonstrably non-democratic present.

Democratic Realism

It is in their willingness to engage with this 'less-than-democratic' side of modern, mass politics that democratic realists distinguish themselves from their idealist counterparts. However, they do so not by posing the difficult, but necessary questions that emerge from a deeper awareness of popular powerlessness, but by considering this focus on powerlessness itself a kind of mistake. In other words, the issue is not that ordinary citizens are politically insignificant, but that we continue to imagine that they could be, or even should be, otherwise. Instead, democratic realists like Gaetano Mosca, Robert Michels, Vilfredo Pareto, Max Weber, Joseph Schumpter, E. E. Schattschneider, and, more recently, Christopher Achen and Larry Bartels argue that democracy does not depend on substantive values like popular sovereignty or political equality, but only a set of procedural mechanisms by which candidates for office are selected "by means of a competitive struggle for the people's vote."[27] As noted briefly in the preceding chapter, this position renders the idea of post-democracy theoretically incoherent; if political institutions are not intended to realize a set of values, then it does not make sense to describe their inability to do so as a failure. Rather, the failure would seem to be on the part of those who ascribe such values; those expecting, for instance, competitive elections to produce something like popular sovereignty in the first place. As such, democratic realists treat the "problem" of post-democracy, to the extent that it constitutes a problem at all, as the result of a simple misunderstanding: that the People were never meant to govern themselves, but only to passively and haphazardly choose those who will.

As such, the main issue is that ordinary citizens still continue to believe in what Schumpeter, Schattschneider, and Achen and Bartels call "the classical doctrine," "the classical theory," or "the folk theory of democracy," respectively.[28] As Achen and Bartels explain, this is broadly the idea that

> Ordinary people have preferences about what their government should do. They choose leaders who will do those things, or they enact their preferences directly in referendums. In either case, what the majority wants becomes government policy... Democracy makes the people the rulers, and legitimacy derives from their consent.[29]

Instead, democratic realists caution us to chasten our view of democratic possibility; namely, to jettison assumptions of popular sovereignty and political equality in favor of a procedural understanding of democracy, one based solely on the availability of competitive elections. Anything more puts an unnecessary onus on what democracy can or should be, leading to confusion and frustration. Schattschneider makes this point clear when writing,

> The great deficiency of American democracy is intellectual, the lack of a good usable definition. A good definition might shed a flood of light on modern politics; it might clarify a thousand muddy concepts and might help us to understand where we are going and what we want. It might even help us get rid of the impossible imperatives that haunt the literature of the subject and give everyone a sense of guilt ... We become cynical about democracy because the public does not act the way the simplistic definition of democracy says that it should act, or we try to whip the public into doing things it does not want to do, is unable to do and has too much sense to do. The crisis here is not a crisis in democracy but a crisis in theory.[30]

Thus, ordinary citizens and researchers alike should embrace a realist perspective and accept elections for what they are: a messy, manipulated, inconclusive poll of how often uninformed, if not misinformed voters feel on a particular day, assuming they have the time and resources to provide an answer.

While perhaps capable of alleviating some guilt, the realist position raises the more fundamental question as to why anyone would value this sort of democracy in the first place. In other words, who would *value* living in a realist democracy, one knowingly subject to the whims of a reactive and injudicious public that, as Achen and Bartels point out, does not promote but actually hinders responsive government?[31] Anticipating this question, Achen and Bartels offer five considerable arguments in its favor. First, they stress, "elections provide authoritative, widely accepted agreement about who shall rule," giving the governing party the legitimacy they need to exercise sovereignty.[32] Second, this process further allows for electoral turnover, preventing any one individual or group from dominating that society.[33] This turnover, third, provides opposition groups with an incentive to tolerate what they may perceive to be poor or unjust rule. "The notion that

50 Idealism, Realism, and Acknowledgment

citizens can oppose the incumbent rulers and organize to replace them yet remain loyal to the nation," they point out, "is fundamental both to real democracy and to social harmony."[34] Fourth, citing John Stuart Mill and others, Achen and Bartels point out that political participation can "have important implications for civic competence and other virtues"; in short, improving the moral character of the citizenry.[35] And finally, the need to seek re-election means that "politicians in well-functioning democracies will strive to avoid being caught violating consensual ethical norms in their society," ultimately enabling the public to police elite behavior.[36]

Under the best of circumstances, it certainly seems like democratic electoral systems should be able to achieve the sorts of benefits described by Achen and Bartels. Elites may still behave boorishly and get away with it and historically marginalized groups (or those who merely consider themselves marginalized) may, at times, still resort to violence, but the legitimacy bestowed by free elections appears invaluable, even when those elections, due either to voter disenfranchisement, successful misinformation campaigns, or shadowy donors, are recognized as less than free. However, without the real possibility of popular sovereignty or political equality, the justifications given by Achen and Bartels are less an argument for democracy than an argument for the appearance of democracy. Responding to a similar set of arguments made by Werner Becker over two decades prior, Habermas makes clear the way in which this sort of democratic realism necessitates a performative contradiction on the part of the citizenry.[37] While from an outsider's perspective, Habermas argues, there may be good reason for valuing and pursuing legitimacy, turnover, toleration, civic virtue, and elite constraints, achieving these benefits requires that actual participants somehow ignore or dismiss the passive, instrumental role they play in politics and, despite it all, continue to involve themselves anyway.

The first three benefits—legitimacy, turnover, and toleration—work only because citizens assume that the ballot is an extension of popular sovereignty, that electoral outcomes represent something more than randomness.[38] Without the belief that voting is an adequate means of representing the public interest, it is unclear why ordinary citizens would continue to vote or engage in any other formal political activity, further losing out on the virtuous benefits that come from regular political participation. The exception would, of course, be those who do stand to gain politically, often regardless of the outcome, that is, the wealthy, those who already do participate the most.[39] Lastly, without informed oversight, the public is only able to punish politicians for the sort of private ethical failings it can readily recognize (e.g., embezzlement, prostitution, possession of illegal narcotics), while more significant policy decisions, such as those made without regard for the public interest (e.g., environmental pollution, privatization, criminalization of behavior), remain unaddressed. In this sense, the advantages listed by Achen and Bartels can only be realized if ordinary citizens reject the foundational premise of the realist position and continue to believe or act as if elections are, in fact, an expression of popular sovereignty and political equality.

Much like post-democracy, democratic realism depends on there still being true believers; without them, there would be no one to participate in the pseudo-democratic practices instrumental for legitimacy, turnover, and so on. More surprisingly, however, is that while post-democracy treats this ongoing faith in democracy as an inevitable product of historical artifact and cultural inertia, democratic realists regularly attack this attachment as confused and misguided. In other words, they want ordinary citizens to recognize the reality of their political situation, but fail to consider how such a broader awareness would necessarily undermine the system they defend. Unable to provide a sufficient normative alternative that stands on its own, democratic realism remains parasitic on the very "folk theory" it seeks to dispel. Achen and Bartels seem to admit as much when, in highlighting that the incentive to tolerate opposition is "fundamental ... to real democracy," they appear to suggest that real democracy is still possible, perhaps that it could even coexist with the realist model of democracy they present.[40]

We could perhaps imagine a more self-aware citizenry, one disinterested in democratic values, but still invested in the benefits Achen and Bartels describe. Thus, rather than tolerating democracy's absence as a kind of open secret (arguably, as many already do), they would think of their continued participation solely as a means of maintaining the noble lie that popular sovereignty and political equality really exist. These citizens would have to participate well aware that their efforts will not have any effect on politics, at least in any sort of intentional or reasoned sense, knowing not simply that their individual vote counts for little or that their candidate may lose, but that the electoral system itself rests on a lie. Under these conditions, the best that could be hoped for is an enlightened despotism or, perhaps, avoiding a debased one, all while having no real say over the matter. This, of course, raises the question of who such a noble lie would be for; if ordinary citizens are able to embrace democratic realism, perhaps by adopting some sort of conservative class consciousness in which they 'know their place,' why not simply extol the benefits of competitive oligarchy, hierarchy, and patronage instead?[41]

At best, democratic realism gives us a model of legitimacy predicated on continued participation, but all without being able to justify that participation beyond the legitimacy it produces. When it comes to questions of membership, responsibility, or culpability, it gives us considerably less. If citizens cannot be described as a People who govern, who are they? Joint participants in an essentially randomized selection process for elites? Those united by the desire to preserve either the myth of democracy or the hollow ritual of election? Or two groups, one aware and the other mystified? And what would citizens owe such a state? Owe to one another? Or owe to victims of state violence or exploitative policymaking?

Ultimately, democratic realism's inability to confront the problem of political powerlessness stems from its unwillingness to treat a fundamental belief in popular sovereignty and political equality as anything more than a mistake. In this way,

52 Idealism, Realism, and Acknowledgment

democratic realists miss the real and enduring significance these values hold for people who grow up within a democratic political culture. They play an integral role in structuring not only how people think about politics and the state, but how they think about their relationship to their broader community, their fellow citizens, and, as Joanna Cook et al. point out, even themselves. They write that

> [democracy] by necessity makes the way in which that sovereignty is realized— and thus the subject's relationship to others and to "the political"—stand out as an explicit object of reflection and anxiety. This is further compounded by democracy's promise that the subject has the capacity to change the political, should she wish. "What am I for the political?" and "What is the political for me?" are thus questions that continually recur for the inhabitant of a democratic system, unlike those living in more feudal or patrimonial systems, where, although such reflection is of course possible, the particular forms of political subjectivity involved deflect sustained reflection away from the constructed notions of the political.[42]

In other words, democratic citizens are not only normatively committed, but practically habituated to thinking of themselves as such, making it both difficult and undesirable to simply cast off these values in favor of a more realist perspective. *Contra* Schattschneider, post-democracy is not merely a crisis in theory, but a crisis in value. Any account which does not address the normative repercussions of democracy's absence fails to adequately grapple with the problem of powerlessness at the heart of post-democracy.

While not democratic realists per se, both Rancière and Wolin's responses to post-democracy fall within this category. Each focuses, not on the subject-centered implications of non-democracy, but only on the way in which the state and modern political life seem to inherently obstruct democratic possibility. In Rancière's case, because he conceives of democracy not as an exercise, but as a disruption of sovereign power, the very idea of popular sovereignty, at least in state form, becomes contradictory.[43] Thus, the modern liberal state has always been post-democratic, a means of imagined consensus that thwarts real democratic conflicts, which only exist at the margins.[44] Wolin agrees, arguing

> that any conception of democracy grounded in the citizen-as-actor and politics-as-episodic is incompatible with the modern choice of the State as the fixed center of political life ... Democracy in the late modern world cannot be a complete political system, and given the awesome potentialities of modern forms of power and what they exact of the social and natural world, it ought not to be hoped or striven for.[45]

He famously introduces the idea of fugitive democracy, further emphasizing the degree to which authentic democratic practice is inherently fleeting.[46] Both

Idealism, Realism, and Acknowledgment **53**

recognize the extent to which the state monopolizes democratic possibility, asking citizens instead to explore non-traditional or informal avenues for the exercise of political power.

While certainly insightful, neither position helps us to further engage with the ongoing consequences of an otherwise, by-and-large, non-democratic existence. Citizens may be open to political action, perhaps even radical action, but to the extent that such actions are rare (as Wolin makes clear), if not purely hypothetical, how should these citizens imagine themselves in the meantime? Political actors lying in wait? Democratic sleeper cells? This position may seem appealing to a select group of democratic partisans, eager to set things right, but neither Rancière nor Wolin give any indication that things can be set right, suggesting rather that democracy may be doomed to be an eternal cycle of boom and bust, something won and lost, the former substantially less often than the latter. One could, nevertheless, remain a Sisyphean democrat, shouldering the boulder of democratic responsibility, come what may. Here, Wolin and Rancière appear much closer to Norval. But again, the same objection emerges: How many citizens are so stalwart, so dedicated to the ever-present possibility of democracy to be able to think of themselves exclusively in these terms? What of the desperate feelings, intrinsic to post-democracy, that democracy has been lost, that the state has failed its citizens, and that citizens have failed each other? How are citizens to reconcile these justifiable feelings with a broader conception of their quotidian political existence?

Acknowledging Post-Democracy

The problem of post-democracy is not one of strategy or tactics, nor is it a kind of deep-seated confusion as to what democracy really means. Rather, it is the problem of coming to terms with an enduring political powerlessness; specifically, doing so in a cultural context that trains citizens to believe such powerlessness to be intolerable, and thus unsustainable, if not impossible. This means taking powerlessness as a brute fact, considering it fully in all of its implications for how citizens relate to the state, their fellow citizens, and themselves, despite all of the temptation and opportunity to avoid it. These opportunities may come in the form of a democratic false consciousness, but more likely (for readers of this book), the ever-present, dimly self-conscious fantasy of democratic citizenship. Even among those willing to broach the topic of democratic decline, the tendency—as we have seen—is either to focus one's efforts exclusively toward democratic possibility and pursuing a better future or to attempt to define away the problem, reducing the matter to a question of semantics by arguing that democracy never was what everyone always considered it to be. All in all, hardly anyone seems interested in exploring the disappointing, yet logical repercussions of a non-democratic present, leaving us with, at best, an inchoate, fragmented conception of post-democratic citizenship.

54 Idealism, Realism, and Acknowledgment

This is not to argue that citizens must *accept* their powerlessness, considering it fair, warranted, or otherwise normatively tolerable. Nor does it suggest that citizens should actively refrain from political action, abstaining from the rare or privileged opportunities to exercise influence when they arise. It is, rather, to argue that citizens must recognize, if not necessarily their powerlessness, then the powerlessness of the vast majority of their fellow citizens. This means, first and foremost, refusing to entertain the fantasy that they live in a democratic state or that they, themselves, are democratic citizens in any meaningful sense of the term. Even among those who do exercise a degree of political power, this means acknowledging that they do so uniquely and under non-democratic conditions; they are not representatives of the People, but merely one more party trying to rule them, even if they presume to do so in the People's interest.

It also means transforming how political theorists and citizens alike conceptualize both the practice of political theory and the ongoing opportunities for political involvement within post-democratic society. For political elites and activists, this shift is significant, but not profound: a general reconsideration of democratic norms of action in light of their inapplicability to the present circumstances. After all, why play by the rules of a broken system? For instance, activists may want to ask themselves whether they owe the broader public a say in—or even the truth of—their efforts. If the People do not actually govern, then perhaps their assent or involvement proves an unnecessary and unfair expectation, especially when comparing 'grassroots' activists with better organized, better financed parties, which often pursue their interests both surreptitiously and ruthlessly. While this may appear to give license to those who wish to abuse their ostensibly democratic power, it is essential to remember that the power they wield at present—in a context devoid of popular sovereignty or political equality—cannot adequately be described as democratic in the first place. Moreover, the persistent expectation that political actors continue to abide by these norms will unduly be felt by those most invested in the public good, uniquely hampering their efforts and putting them at a further disadvantage when competing with less scrupulous political elites. Ultimately, this suggests that willing, capable parties spend less time reading democratic theory and more time reading Machiavelli, Clausewitz, and Sun Tzu.

But what of the rest, those citizens who at most exercise a superficial degree of power, those too preoccupied or simply unable to become the sort of politically active citizens they otherwise aspire to be? They require a radically different approach to both political theory and the sort of (pseudo-)political participation indicative of post-democratic life, one which sees such practices, not as a chance to transform the conditions of their powerlessness, but to confront and, in the end, weather them. Here both interpretation (theory) and action (participation) are not political in themselves, but therapeutic. The aim is not to influence law or state policy—which, at present, remains unrealistic—but instead to privately respond to the influence exercised by others.

In the next chapter, we explore the background, greater consequences, and import of a therapeutic approach to political philosophy, showing how political philosophy has and can enable citizens to work through the broader implications of post-democratic political life. This will set the stage for a post-democratic reading of the work of Thomas Hobbes (Chapter Five), in which we will begin to construct a comprehensive model of post-democratic citizenship, one which offers a framework for thinking about legitimacy, membership, responsibility, and culpability more appropriate to a context which lacks both popular sovereignty and political equality. Finally, in Chapter Six, we will conclude by surveying the ways in which participation in (pseudo-)political practices like voting, discussion, and protest can themselves serve a therapeutic purpose, a way of further engaging with the political powerlessness at the heart of post-democracy. Together, these three chapters form an initial foray into a desperately needed study of post-democratic life.

Notes

1. Hook 1974, pp. 13–16
2. This effect may not be immediate and is certainly not guaranteed, but the intention is enough to qualify the work as idealist.
3. Willis 2015, p. 202
4. Rorty 2004, p. 11
5. Habermas 2012, pp. 49, 51–52
6. Crouch 2004, p. 110
7. Crouch 2004, pp. 112–116
8. Crouch 2004, p. 122
9. Crouch 2004, p. 120
10. Crouch 2004, p. 111
11. Crouch 2004, p. 122
12. Crouch 2004, pp. 19–21
13. Crouch 2004, p. 104
14. Crouch 2004, p. 104
15. Habermas 2012, p. 52
16. Habermas 2012, p. 12
17. Rorty 2004, p. 11
18. Honig 2001, pp. 117–118
19. Honig 2001, p. 118
20. Rorty 1998, pp. 10–11, quoted in Honig 2001, p. 116
21. Honig 2001, pp. 114–115
22. Norval 2007, pp. 145–147
23. Norval 2007, p. 4
24. Derrida 2005, p. 85, quoted in Norval 2007, p. 146
25. Norval 2007, pp. 196–199
26. On Augustinian authoritarianism, see Connolly 1993. On Nietzschean elitism, see Beiner 2018.
27. Schumpeter [1942] 1954, p. 269. See Mosca [1896] 1939, Michels [1911] 1962, Pareto [1920] 2017, Weber [1922] 1978, Schattschneider 1960, Achen and Bartels 2016.
28. Schumpeter [1942] 1954, ch. XXI; Schattschneider 1960, ch. 8; Achen and Bartels 2016, ch. 1

56 Idealism, Realism, and Acknowledgment

29 Achen and Bartels 2016, p. 1
30 Schattschneider 1960, pp. 131, 134
31 Achen and Bartels 2016, pp. 311–316
32 Achen and Bartels 2016, p. 317
33 Achen and Bartels 2016, p. 317
34 Achen and Bartels 2016, pp. 317–318. When combined, these first three arguments yield an additional, invaluable benefit, one left unmentioned by Achen and Bartels: the prevention of (or at least discouragement of) politically-motivated violence.
35 Achen and Bartels 2016, p. 318. See also Constant [1819] 1988, pp. 308–328.
36 Achen and Bartels 2016, p. 318
37 Habermas [1992] 1998, pp. 289–295
38 Achen and Bartels 2016, pp. 175–176
39 This is not to say that the wealthy's electoral experience is in any sense less random (e. g. Brexit, 2016 Presidential Election), only that all possible outcomes are typically in their favor.
40 Achen and Bartels 2016, p. 318
41 One could further imagine an esoteric theory of democratic realism, one in which the truth of democracy's absence is restricted to a tiny elite, those who understand either liberalism or oligarchy's existential dependence on an ornamental democracy. This hardly seems to be Achen or Bartel's aim, but to the extent that most citizens continue to unreflectively participate in politics, it may provide a more functional explanation. Yet, this still raises the question as to how the rest of us, those who recognize its ornamental quality but fail to be convinced of its benefits, should engage with the ongoing political powerlessness democratic realism defends.
42 Cook et al. 2016, pp. 7–8
43 Rancière [1995] 1999, p. 99
44 Rancière [1995] 1999, pp. 139–140
45 Wolin 1994, p. 23
46 Wolin 1994

References

Achen, Christopher H. and Larry Bartels. *Democracy for Realists: Why Elections Do Not Produce Responsive Government*. Princeton, NJ: Princeton UP, 2016.

Beiner, Ronald. *Nietzsche, Heidegger, and the Return of the Far Right*. Philadelphia: University of Pennsylvania Press, 2018.

Connolly, William E. *The Augustinian Imperative: A Reflection on the Politics of Morality*. New York: Sage Press, 1993.

Constant, Benjamin. "The Liberty of the Ancients Compared with that of the Moderns" in *Political Writings*. Biancamaria Fontana, ed. New York: Cambridge UP, [1819] 1988.

Cook, Joanna, Nicholas J. Long, and Henrietta L. Moore. "Introduction: When Democracy 'Goes Wrong'" in *The State We're In: Reflecting on Democracy's Troubles*. Cook, Joanna, Nicholas J. Long, and Henrietta L. Moore, eds. New York: Berghahn Books, 2016.

Crouch, Colin. *Post-Democracy*. Malden, MA: Polity Press, 2004.

Derrida, Jacques. *Rogues: Two Essays on Reason*. Redwood City, CA: Stanford UP, 2005.

Habermas, Jurgen. *Between Facts and Norms: Contributions to a Discourse Theory of Law and Democracy*. Cambridge, MA: MIT Press, [1992] 1998.

Habermas, Jurgen. *The Crisis of the European Union: A Response*. Malden, MA: Polity Press, 2012.

Honig, Bonnie. *Democracy and The Foreigner*. Princeton, NJ: Princeton UP, 2001.

Hook, Sidney. *Pragmatism and the Tragic Sense of Life*. New York: Basic Books Inc, 1974.

Michels, Robert. *Political Parties: A Sociological Study of the Oligarchical Tendencies of Modern Democracy.* New York: The Free Press, [1911] 1962.

Mosca, Gaetano. *The Ruling Class.* New York: McGraw-Hill, [1896] 1939.

Norval, Aletta J. *Aversive Democracy: Inheritance and Originality in the Democratic Tradition.* New York: Cambridge UP, 2007.

Pareto, Vilfredo. *The Rise and Fall of Elites: An Application of Theoretical Sociology.* New York: Routledge Press, [1920] 2017.

Rancière, Jacques. *Dis-agreement: Politics and Philosophy.* Minneapolis, MN: University of Minnesota Press, [1995] 1999.

Rorty, Richard. *Achieving Our Country: Leftist Thought in Twentieth-Century America.* Cambridge, MA: Harvard UP, 1998.

Rorty, Richard. "Post-Democracy: Richard Rorty on Anti-Terrorism and the National Security State," *London Review of Books* 26. 7 (April 1, 2004): 10–11.

Schattschneider, E. E.The Semisovereign People: A Realist's view of Democracy in America. New York: Holt, Rhinehart, and Winston, 1960.

Schumpeter, Joseph. *Capitalism, Socialism, and Democracy.* New York: Ruskin House, [1942] 1954.

Weber, Max. *Economy and Society.* Berkeley, CA: University of California Press, [1922] 1978.

Willis, Andre C. "Considering 'Post-Democracy'," *Juncture* 22. 3 (Winter 2015): 201–202.

Wolin, Sheldon. "Fugitive Democracy," *Constellations* 1. 1 (December 1994): 11–25.

4

POST-DEMOCRATIC POLITICAL PHILOSOPHY

Engaging with the broader implications of post-democracy requires acknowledging the enduring conditions of political inequality and general powerlessness that characterize political life in an otherwise nominal democracy. There are some exceptions; economic elites, politicians, and activists still exercise forms of political power, but even they act on an uneven playing field, where wealth plays an integral, if not decisive role, while the vast majority of citizens remain on the sidelines. These conditions have consequences, not only for the substantive beliefs citizens hold about the state, their fellow citizens, and the idea of citizenship, but for the theoretical approaches citizens employ to arrive at those substantive beliefs; namely, the questions they pose, what motivates these questions, and what counts as justification. In other words, we must examine the way in which a post-democratic diagnosis would affect both citizens' conceptions about politics and *how* they conceptualize politics, that is, the practice of political philosophy itself.

Thus, it is essential that this approach does not fall back into democratic habits by assuming that the citizen's motivation for re-imagining citizenship should be, either once again or for the first time, to exercise political influence; that is, to become democratic citizens. Such thinking, while familiar and, hence, understandable, encourages the citizen to evade any further reflection on the conditions of powerlessness they experience. Rather, in order to think through post-democracy on its own terms, citizens must be willing to reconcile themselves with their general lack of political significance. In this sense, the post-democratic approach to political philosophy primarily seeks to elaborate a 'guide for the governed,' an account of political activity and authority relevant for the nominal citizen, the Aristotelian mechanic of the 21st century, which is to say, those of us who work (outside of politics) for a living.[1] This is done not in order to legitimate post-democratic sovereignty or produce more obedient subjects, which would be in the interest of the state alone. Rather, this confrontation is necessary to better understand the post-democratic experience, to clarify one's feelings toward it, and to respond in such a way that mitigates the frustration, anxiety, and alienation that accompanies the awareness of a non-democratic political existence. In short, to find a way to live with it.

This chapter defends a uniquely post-democratic interpretation of political philosophy, one which aims to help the bewildered democratic citizen better recognize and work through the confusions and complications engendered by the politico-cultural contradictions of post-democratic life. In this sense, the practice of political philosophy assumes an essentially therapeutic character. After first exploring why post-democracy invites such an interpretation, this chapter will lay the groundwork for a therapeutic approach to political philosophy: an approach which prioritizes the well-being of the ruled over the question of rule. This chapter will conclude by contrasting the post-democratic interpretation of political philosophy developed here with two other recent responses to political limitation; specifically, Joshua For Dienstag's political pessimism and Jeffrey Green's Epicurean defense of extrapoliticism.[2] Ultimately, by showing how Green's democratic orientation limits the value of his prescriptions, I will elucidate why therapeutically engaging with post-democracy requires adopting a post-democratic model of citizenship (presented in Chapter Five) as one's own.

Fear and Loathing under Post-Democracy

To be a democratic citizen is to think as a political actor, to think of oneself as able to actively and intentionally influence sovereign decision-making. Thus, politics is not simply a question of how one is governed, but of how one governs oneself, of how a given community, a 'we,' exercises its collective autonomy. Thus, democratic citizens, in addition to adopting a particular disposition toward politics, are predisposed to think of themselves as *inherently political*, to consider their political status existentially significant. Their relationship to politics, in other words, is not something superfluous or tangential to their sense of self, but constitutive of it.

Of course, not all self-understood democratic citizens feel as deep an attachment to politics. It is not difficult to find those who profess to cherish democratic practice, yet fail to give actual political activity a second thought. We might call these individuals *Humean citizens*.[3] David Hume, the 18th-century Scottish philosopher, famously critiqued the early modern social contract tradition on the basis that citizens do not base their attachment to the state on any actual or ongoing contract between them, but on the ways of life to which they are habituated.[4] "Time and custom give authority to all forms of government, and all successions of princes," he argues, "and that power, which at first was founded only on injustice and violence, becomes in time legal and obligatory."[5] For

60 Post-Democratic Political Philosophy

Humean citizens, the absence of democratic political practice proves to be insignificant; what is essential is not the ability to exercise political influence, but the social rituals to which they are accustomed. Their relationship to political authority and activity is not predicated on a particular *political* self-understanding, but on an exclusively cultural one. Hence, rather than ruminate on the consequences of post-democratic sovereignty, they would find "no maxim ... more conformable, both to prudence and morals, than to submit quietly to the government which we find established in the country where we happen to live."[6]

As such, to the Humean citizen, a post-democratic diagnosis would seem largely unimportant. Rather, like the self-aware realist dismissed in Chapter Three, these citizens never expected to exercise popular sovereignty, but only to enjoy the practices (e.g., voting, discussion, rallies) associated with its presumed exercise. Unlike those who succumb to the fantasy of democratic citizenship, these would be citizens who willingly assume a sort of ironic disposition toward politics, one in which citizens continue to embrace the democratic imaginary with which they are familiar, doing so in full knowledge that their efforts are insignificant and largely symbolic. In a context that puts such a pervasive emphasis on political identity, this sort of detachment can make one appear insincere, if not disingenuous. For instance, it would require only discussing politics superficially or, when voting, to do so without any sort of serious or intentional consideration, but well-aware of how little it matters. Ultimately, because post-democratic citizens are so regularly treated *as if* they were democratic citizens, any sort of consistent, ironic response would necessarily take the form of an endless satire at the expense of those around them, a form of pretend in which no one else is in on the joke.

Yet, for most, post-democratic life is so tied to a democratic political imaginary that it would be impossible to disentangle the real exercise of political power from social custom. In other words, post-democratic citizens are not simply habituated to democratic rituals, but to thinking of themselves as actually exercising political power, even if they have never actually done so. In fact, it is precisely this ubiquitous 'call to politics' that makes the prospect of post-democracy so traumatic. It consistently reminds the individual that the failure to realize popular sovereignty and political equality is, rather than something to be nonchalantly sloughed off, precisely that: a *failure*. Moreover, it is not merely a societal failing, but *their own*. As democratic citizens, they should be able to use their power to prevent the corruption of democratic practice or, at the very least, to right the ship when corruption becomes evident. Yet, the open persistence of a non-democratic status quo highlights their inability to do so, endlessly underscoring their general political negligibility. The myriad of ways in which they continue to be addressed as democratic citizens, invited to take responsibility for conditions and decisions they are unable to affect, only exacerbate their feelings of defeat and disappointment. They are, in short, reminded daily of their powerlessness.

Nevertheless, there will always be those who find ways of ignoring these conditions (e.g., the Humean, the generally apathetic, the blissfully unaware); post-democracy depends on them. But what of those unable to do so? How, then, would they experience a realization of post-democratic citizenship, of internalizing democracy's absence while enveloped in a culture that tirelessly evokes and celebrates its presence? While such experiences are inherently unique, conditioned by other politically-relevant factors (e.g., gender, race, class, sexuality, etc.) that may, often unpredictably, soften or intensify one's response to post-democracy, we can identify three broad consequences of adopting a post-democratic orientation: frustration, anxiety, and alienation.

Accustomed to thinking of themselves as democratic citizens, we should expect post-democratic citizens to become frustrated over their inability to influence political outcomes or, subsequently, to realize democratic ideals. The consistent discursive emphasis on democratic values and the availability of mechanisms that should, ostensibly, allow for their realization (e.g., free elections, free speech, right to organize, etc.) only serve to compound these feelings, impeding the citizen's ability to 'move on' from the mirage of democratic possibility. While unpleasant in itself, the greater consequences of this frustration, however, will inevitably depend on the way they conceptualize its roots, for example whether they blame the state, capitalism, the wealthy, or another external, empowered institution or group, real or imagined, for rendering them politically insignificant. This has the further potential to breed deep feelings of institutional distrust or resentment, perhaps even the sense that they are being persecuted. If they instead (or additionally) find fault with their fellow citizens, holding their ignorance or apathy responsible for their collective failure, this may lead to a more general feeling of antipathy toward their society, even neighbors. Additionally, they may direct blame inward, at their own inability to affect political change, and become disappointed in—if not ashamed of—themselves.

While post-democratic citizens experience frustration over their failure to become political actors, they further suffer anxiety over what appears to be an uncertain future, one in which they lack any influence over political outcomes. Though genuinely democratic citizens may become anxious over a particular political decision or election, it remains tempered by the sense that they continue to have a 'seat at the table'; as such, the demos always has the ability to intervene before (or, at the very least, once) the state does anything truly terrible. Yet, under post-democracy, that assumption is no longer tenable. Rather, citizens must confront the fact that the state is not beholden to them at all, either as an individual or a member of the demos. While there are still some checks on state power (e.g., elite influence, 'the bureaucracy,' etc.), these checks are still radically divorced from their own influence, instead acting in their own, private interest. At best, all they can hope for is that their interests and those of the powerful overlap. All of this contributes to a deep-seated disquiet concerning sovereign power. And while post-democratic sovereignty hardly guarantees that something

62 Post-Democratic Political Philosophy

horrible will happen, it does leave citizens with the impression that they would be unable to prevent it, leading them to feel distressed, insecure, and trapped.

Ultimately, this combination of frustration and anxiety contributes to a profound sense of alienation, not only from political activity, but from one's fellow citizens as well. On face, the recognition of political powerlessness distances post-democratic citizens from both sovereign power and the various institutions connected to it. No longer able to see these institutions as an extension of their will or, at the very least, subject to it, they may come to see the power held by those institutions as arbitrary and illegitimate, estranging them from the forces that structure and condition their daily existence.

Furthermore, a post-democratic outlook may separate citizens from their neighbors as well. On one level, they can no longer imagine a connection with others based on their shared participation in political activity; they have ceased to be 'fellow citizens.' On another, living amongst a population seemingly blind to their own political status, continuing to revel in the fantasy of democratic practice, can leave aware post-democratic citizens feeling even more isolated. The consistent talk of democratic participation and civic responsibility, whether in public discourse or private conversation, has the potential to disaffect them further, turning them into a sort of Cassandra figure surrounded by blithe Trojans, except, of course, that the post-democratic citizen's claim is not prophetic, but manifest. All of this serves to isolate the post-democratic citizen, leaving them both politically and epistemically alone.

None of this paints a post-democratic perspective in a particularly flattering light. Excluding those instances in which a post-democratic regime explicitly threatens individual liberty or shows contempt for expertise, it would be much easier to approach post-democracy from a liberal or technocratic perspective, indifferent to the absence of democratic practice. This indifference, however, may be harder to cultivate than one realizes. In addition to growing up in a culture that ubiquitously celebrates democratic values, many self-aware post-democratic citizens continue to embrace democratic principles, despite being pessimistic about their realization. In short, one does not simply give up on democracy. Thus, while one must decide to adopt a post-democratic orientation, the democratic sympathies underlying that decision are not always a matter of choice. Whether post-democratic citizens choose to engage with their feelings of frustration, anxiety, and alienation directly (e.g., by throwing themselves into democratic activism) or by trying their best not to think about it, these feelings will continue to affect them until they work through them. Thus, what post-democratic citizens need is not more strategy, but therapy.

Philosophy as Therapy

The idea of philosophy as a form of therapy is at least as old as Socrates, who interpreted the aim of philosophy as making "your first and chief concern … the highest welfare of your souls."[7] Following Socrates, it has been associated with figures as diverse as the Stoics, Augustine, Boethius, Montaigne, Rousseau, Emerson, Thoreau, Kierkegaard, Nietzsche, Heidegger, Wittgenstein, and Stanley Cavell.[8] Broadly speaking, what distinguishes this loose assemblage of thinkers as a philosophical tradition is the way they consider both 'the philosophical problem' a source of deep, often existential worry and, subsequently, the practice of philosophy as a means of responding to that worry.

For the most part, people philosophize because they love or enjoy the practice, not because the problem at hand distresses them to the point they feel as if they cannot avoid it. For instance, the majority of people who purposely read Descartes do so out of an interest in epistemology or early modern thought, not because they are experiencing a crisis brought on by a deep concern with the nature of reality. Though there are certainly exceptions, even (or perhaps especially) those who practice philosophy for a living are often motivated more by tenure reviews, reputations, or a general passion for the subject rather than an anxious fixation on a particular problem or set of problems.

Still, there are instances in which one turns to philosophy out of a sort of desperation, a feeling that the world has become unfamiliar or unstable in a way that makes it difficult to continue on as one previously had. These are moments when individuals undergo a profound realization that disrupts their prior ideas about both the world and their relationship to it, leaving them bewildered, unsettled, and unsure of how to respond. Socrates experiences this upon receiving Chaerephon's news that the Oracle of Delphi proclaimed no one wiser than he; Boethius, upon becoming aware of his impending execution; Kierkegaard, upon recognizing the irreconcilability of modern life with Christian virtue; Nietzsche, upon realizing the greater implications of the loss of God; and Emerson, by the feelings of grief and detachment following the death of his son. Without some sort of resolution, these problems can estrange one from the world one inhabits, often leading to feelings of disquiet, dread, even the wholesale rejection of the world, that is, nihilism.

A therapeutic approach to philosophy, then, aims to alleviate such feelings by restoring a sense of familiarity with the world; specifically, by thinking about and contextualizing the philosophical problem in a way that enables the individual to move beyond it. This involves adopting a new framework that facilitates a successful reconciliation with the world, making one's problems seem less vexing or arresting, or even ill-considered, as if they had just not been judged in the right light. James Peterman, writing on Wittgenstein's own form of philosophical therapy, describes this as "bringing about a proper attitude toward the world" or "being in agreement with the world."[9] As Wittgenstein himself explains,

> the clarity that we are aiming at is indeed complete clarity. But this simply means that the philosophical problems should completely disappear. The real discovery is the one that enables me to break off philosophizing when I want to. The one that gives philosophy peace, so that it is no longer tormented by questions which bring itself in question.[10]

64 Post-Democratic Political Philosophy

Thus, the aim of philosophical therapy is not to solve the problem, at least in the sense that one solves a math problem or a crossword puzzle, but to dissolve the problem, to make the problem no longer appear problematic; analogously, to no longer consider the crossword puzzle worth doing.[11]

We see this in Cavell's response to the problem of other minds, of whether one can ever truly know another to be like oneself. Initially, the problem appears to stem from the other (hence, the problem of *other* minds), their essential unknowability. Yet, a further philosophical intervention allows Cavell to see it as an issue, not of epistemic certainty, but of attunement, of withholding oneself; in turn, his interpretation of the problem radically shifts. As Andrew Norris explains, this enables Cavell to show that

> it is we who have fallen away from the world and the other. And we have done so by trying to force them to come to us, by making the world and the others as such objects of knowledge. The truth of skepticism is that of our self-alienation, not of our ignorance.[12]

As a result, Cavell emphasizes,

> all this makes it seem that the philosophical problem of knowledge is something I impose on these matters; that I am the philosophical problem. I am. It is in me that the circuit of communication is cut; I am the stone on which the wheel breaks.[13]

In other words, a philosophical intervention does not respond to a problem out in the world, but inside oneself; it aims, *contra* Marx, not to change the world, but to change one's interpretation of it. No longer vexed with the problem of other minds, Cavell turns to the democratic challenge of collectively realizing a shared community. Unlike that of philosophical skepticism, this problem, Cavell argues, can be solved through our willingness to be responsive to one another.[14] In contrast, the post-democrat has come to accept that Cavell's "eventual human community" will not be found, focusing instead on the consequences of its absence.[15]

Overall, the therapeutic value resulting from philosophical practice comes not from any new framework *per se*, but the process one takes to practically internalize that framework. In Freudian psychoanalysis, this process is called *working-through*, "the process by which a person transforms a relatively theoretical insight into their unconscious motivations into a practical understanding of how they permeate aspects of their lives."[16] Much in the same way one cannot simply decide to no longer feel anxious, this new, salutary understanding must be learned through exploring both the conceptual and practical consequences engendered by this paradigm shift and adapting one's life accordingly. As Peterman emphasizes,

It means living that truth, being at home in it. So to solve philosophical problems requires that one live those solutions. It requires not simply being aware of the truth but also changing one's life. In this context it requires a deep and difficult alteration in one's mode of thinking and expressing oneself.[17]

Thus, one suffering an existential crisis cannot simply pick up a copy of *Being and Time*, read it cover to cover, and expect to feel better, but must work to actively embrace new perspectives on mortality, affectivity, and worldliness that further lead to practical changes in one's life, often in ways that one could not have previously expected. In order to reconcile himself with the pronouncement of the Oracle, Socrates becomes the 'gadfly' that attempts to wake the city of Athens; in responding to the absence of God in modern life, Kierkegaard attempts to become a new kind of Christian subject, whereas Nietzsche attempts to transvaluate all values; and comforting himself over his impending execution, Boethius writes his own consolations.

In this sense, philosophical practice, like any other sort of therapy, necessitates some degree of active self-transformation. What is first considered merely in the abstract must be made concrete through a willingness to modify one's life in light of what one now perceives as true, good, or right. Thus, it is best to understand a therapeutic approach to philosophy as an ethical project, one which seeks to realize a human good—the well-being of the individual—through the cultivation of a new ethos better suited to the world in which one finds oneself. Ideally, the philosophical text functions as a guide for recognizing the problematic assumptions one may have about the world, as well as offering a means of developing a new framework with which to replace them. Still, this is much easier said than done. Even in making a serious effort to philosophically reorient oneself, one may not always be successful, but instead be unable to find a way of being "in agreement the world" while also being agreeable to oneself. Like all other forms of therapy, there are no guarantees that one's problems will be resolved or even abated.

Political Philosophy as Therapy

How, then, should we conceptualize a therapeutic approach to *political* philosophy? James Glass, in his account of Rousseau, suggests that "the doing of therapy for the political philosopher means to think of the therapeutic task as a political event, to assume that the 'sickness' of psyche lies intimately involved with the general degeneration of the culture itself."[18] As with Gilles Deleuze and Felix Guattari's turn to *schizoanalysis*, Glass's account calls for a politicization of psychoanalysis in order to transform psychoanalytic therapy itself into a form of political activity.[19] In contrast, Gertrude Steuernagel interprets the therapeutic approach as an invitation to integrate certain psychological insights into our normative accounts of politics. Writing on Marcuse and Jung, she observes

66 Post-Democratic Political Philosophy

> To conceive of political philosophy as therapy means to be alive to the complex and often intricate demands of internal and external reality. It means being willing to fit the type of political recommendations to the reality we are confronted with rather than trying to impose a series of principles on a community or group of individuals.[20]

In other words, it is to attune one's sense of political judgment with the nature of the human psyche, to psychologize political activity.

Despite their differences, both Glass and Steuernagel subordinate the therapeutic task to the question of politics; therapy either becomes a means of ameliorating a corrupt society or instrumental for developing better prescriptions for doing so. In prioritizing the question of politics over 'the welfare of one's soul,' Glass and Steuernagel's interpretations thus break with the greater tradition of philosophy as therapy. In their work, the issue is not that one has become estranged from the world and must find a new way of reconciling oneself with it, but instead that one is familiar with an evil or broken world and must find a way to change it. The goal then becomes cultivating the best disposition for bringing about a new or different kind of world; in short, to exercise political influence. While there is nothing wrong in principle with Glass and Steuernagel's conception of *political* therapy, it ultimately holds little appeal for the post-democratic citizen, who is neither able to play the role of the politically motivated analyst nor to realize psychologically informed political prescriptions.

What is required, then, is a means of engaging in political *therapy*, a way of finding agreement with a political context out of joint with one's previous assumptions and expectations. There is some precedent for this sort of approach, found largely among the Romans. During the collapse of the Republic, a large swath of the ruling class similarly had to grapple with the unanticipated experience of political inconsequentiality, particularly during the more brutal periods of the Empire. As a result, Ciceroian appeals to save the Republic soon gave way to other, more self-reflexive responses to life under despotism.[21] For instance, Seneca's *De Otio* defends resigning from political life in the event one either lives in an unjust commonwealth or simply has more important tasks (such as philosophy) to which to attend.[22] Tacitus's *Agricola*, detailing the life of his father-in-law, offers an account of how best to serve a violent, tyrannical Emperor without getting oneself killed or compromising one's integrity.[23] Finally, Epictetus expounded a cosmopolitan model of citizenship that philosophically relegated the authority of the citadel by prioritizing one's greater relationship to the *cosmos*.[24]

Michel Foucault famously describes the Romans as collectively responding to

> a crisis of the subject, or rather crisis of subjectivation … a difficulty in the manner in which the individual could form himself as the ethical subject of his actions, and efforts to find in devotion to self that which could enable him to submit to rules and give a purpose to his existence.[25]

No longer able to assume the Senatorial powers (or other positions of political influence) held by their fathers and grandfathers, they had to recalibrate their political self-conceptions; however, because the Empire remained such a fundamental part of their lives, simple withdrawal was not a realistic option. Rather, they had to "elaborat[e] an ethics that enabled one to constitute oneself as an ethical subject with respect to these social, civic, and political activities, in the different forms they might take and at whatever distance one remained from them."[26] Thus, even if, like Seneca, one ultimately decides upon withdrawal, it must be a principled or reasoned withdrawal, one which responds to the prevailing assumption that one should always participate in political activity, despite its hazards. By providing some measure of direction and virtue in otherwise uncertain and/or wicked times, this sort of philosophically guided self-reflection allowed individuals to, as the title of Foucault's work alludes, care for themselves.

More recently, Jonathan Lear's *Radical Hope: Ethics in the Face of Cultural Devastation* gives us an exemplary account of this approach to political philosophy. In it, he describes how Plenty Coups, a chief of the Crow Nation, reimagines the practice of counting coup and, by extension, the warrior way of life native to the Crow, in light of the United States Federal Government's ban on intertribal warfare. Following the ban, as well as the extermination of the buffalo, the Crow lost the ability to engage in the activities essential to their identity *as Crow*. Consequently, nothing seemed to make sense or matter anymore; as Plenty Coups describes it, "After that, nothing happened."[27] Taking the Crow's perspective, Lear writes,

> My problem is not simply that my way of life has come to an end. I no longer have concepts with which to understand myself or the world ... I have no *idea* what is going on. This is not primarily a psychological problem. The concepts with which I would otherwise have understood myself — indeed, the concepts with which I would otherwise have shaped my identity — have gone out of existence.[28]

In other words, the Crow's form of life became unintelligible, leaving them both disoriented and hopeless.

In response, Plenty Coups constructed a new narrative, one which recounted a dream of a receptive Chickadee and "gave the tribe imaginative tools with which to endure a conceptual onslaught."[29] Despite having no idea what the future would bring, the Crow resolved to adapt to whatever changes they would be forced to endure, to become who they needed to become in order to survive, even if that meant diluting or altering their traditions. As such, "they explicitly recognized in an official council that their buffalo-hunting way of life was coming to an end, and they decided to ally with the white man against their traditional enemies."[30] Lear credits decisions like these with ultimately leading to better outcomes than those experienced by other tribes less willing to accept their catastrophic predicament (i.e., the Sioux under Sitting Bull).

68 Post-Democratic Political Philosophy

Through his efforts, Plenty Coups embraced what Lear describes as a vision of radical hope. Broadly, radical hope is

> committed to the bare idea *that something good will emerge*. But it does so in recognition that one's thick understandings of the good life are about to disappear. It thereby manifests a commitment to the idea that the goodness of the world transcends one's limited and vulnerable attempts to understand it … Precisely because Plenty Coups sees that a traditional way of life is coming to an end, he is in a position to embrace a peculiar form of hopefulness. It is basically a hope for *revival*: for coming back to life in a form that is not yet intelligible.[31]

By accepting that the Crow's way of life was no longer tenable, Plenty Coups gave the Crow people a way of moving forward. At that point, it was still unclear what that way forward would be, what Crow life would look like under profoundly different conditions, but by encouraging the tribe to be receptive to a future that still allowed for *some* good, Plenty Coups opened up the possibility for a future worth having. This possibility depended on a willingness to be receptive to an emergent good; specifically, by attuning oneself to a present that appears both strange and undesirable. While this sort of instrumental optimism hardly guarantees that one will find a *better* life, it can help to avoid a life marred by bewilderment and despair.

Post-Democracy and Pessimism

In order to respond to the "crisis of subjectivation" besetting the post-democratic citizen, a philosophical intervention into post-democratic life must be motivated by a similar appreciation of radical hope. Clearly, the devastation suffered by the Crow people differs dramatically from the loss experienced by the post-democratic citizen; clearly, post-democratic citizens are not threatened with genocide. Yet, like the Crow, post-democratic citizens find themselves weathering a "conceptual onslaught" of their own, one in which democratic conceptions of the good are becoming increasingly irrelevant to their contemporary political experience. As such, they must find a way to reconcile themselves with a political context that—while both uncertain and unwelcome—they have few options but to endure.

In this sense, despite espousing Lear's radical hope, the post-democratic approach has a great deal in common with the recent, remarkable elaboration of pessimism offered by Joshua Foa Dienstag. Pessimism, Dienstag tells us, should not be confused with acquiescence or cynicism, but rather a certain weariness toward the idea of infinite or unhindered progress, one informed by the cultural and/or metaphysical conditions of human existence and found in the work of thinkers like Rousseau, Schopenhauer, Nietzsche, Weber, Freud, Adorno,

Foucault, and others.[32] This weariness, he argues, "while it does indeed ask us to limit and eliminate some of our hopes and expectations, it can provide us with the means to better navigate the bounded universe it describes."[33]

How does it do this? By freeing us from our expectations and allowing a more contingent, contextualized relationship with the world as we find it, pessimism enables us to better attend to the problems and possibility of the present. As Dienstag explains,

> Optimism subordinates the present to what is to come and thereby devalues it. Pessimism embodies a free relation to the future. In refraining from hope and prediction we make possible a concern that is not self-abasing and self-pitying. By not holding every moment hostage to its future import, we also make possible a genuinely friendly responsibility to ourselves and to others.[34]

In abstaining from prediction and maintaining "a free relation to the future," Dienstag's position here is not far divorced from Lear's own, with the major exception being that radical hope remains predicated on the belief that something good will emerge, that even if conditions do not change, there are things individuals can do to make life more bearable. In contrast, the pessimist wants, but expects nothing; "they are at rest," Dienstag writes, "but not at home."[35] In other words, the pessimist forgoes even the lingering hope that a better way can be found, at least not for long, instead emphasizing that all achievements are provisional.[36] Lear, for his part, never suggests that the practice of radical hope provides fixed solutions, much less guarantees them, but he does hold on to the possibility that one may again, like the Crow, feel "at home," if only for a little while. Here, the difference may be construed as one of emphasis rather than as a hard distinction, but is nevertheless telling. A pessimist may agree with the post-democrat's diagnosis, but the pessimist would also remain deeply skeptical of the citizenry's ability to better reconcile themselves to post-democracy or, for that matter, even the value of doing so. The aim, rather, is to keep one's eyes open to perennial conditions which limit human possibility; "to teach us to live with what we cannot eradicate, the limitations of death and time with which the universe saddles us."[37]

As Dienstag argues, this focus on limitation enables citizen to both "fortify their souls" against such limitations and remain open to political alternatives that may otherwise be obscured by narrow expectations born of an optimism deeply-rooted in the status quo.[38] In particular, he targets the modern attachment to liberalism, challenging the idea that we should derive "the value of our political liberties from their capacity to allow individuals to pursue a hollow idol of the future."[39] Instead, a pessimistic approach to politics would "defend them in terms of their contribution to the democracy of moments."[40] But what does he mean here by a "democracy of moments"? In an earlier passage, he writes,

70 Post-Democratic Political Philosophy

> Pessimistic freedom is not tied to historical outcomes—neither to national projects nor to personal life-plans. Nor can it be tied to institutional arrangements of noninterference or non-domination. Rather, pessimism envisions a democracy of moments for an individual who can neither escape time but is not imprisoned by it either.[41]

Here, it seems Dienstag is defending a sort of 'fugitive democracy' in which citizens may find contingent, fleeting moments of democratic possibility. Later on, he describes the pessimist as

> in search of a new direction that might claim a day, or a week, or a span of years, and of compatriots with whom to explore that path. A mobile army of meddlers, métiers, anthropomorphizers, in short, a sum of human relations that, viewed from a proper distance, appears as solid as a fleet of ships, or a hornets' nest.[42]

Hence, while pessimists remain cautious not to indulge in the fantasy of lasting success or established coalitions, they continue to seek out opportunities to affect political outcomes, as well as the practical relationships that may facilitate their ability to do so.

Curiously, this faith in the "democracy of moments" emerges as the pessimist's sole moment of optimism. The intrinsic limitations of the human condition and other inescapable cultural and historical elements may thwart any guarantee of happiness and/or freedom, but still the pessimist remains attached to and focused on *democratic* possibility, so much so that at one point Dienstag even declares that "pessimism *is* the democracy of moments."[43] But why should we even assume there will be moments? This deep commitment to democracy, not merely on a normative level, but a descriptive one as well, suggests that democracy is the one expectation with which the pessimist is unwilling to dispense. In this regard, Dienstag's pessimism breaks with the broader theory of post-democracy elaborated in this book. The post-democratic citizen, rather, takes a more pessimistic tack than the pessimists themselves, challenging the pessimists' fixation with democratic possibility—regardless of how limited a duration—in favor of a more thorough examination of the decidedly non-democratic experience of politics at present. In other words, the post-democrat is the pessimist who has run out of political alternatives or, better, no longer wishes to entertain the fantasy of their impending realization, but instead explore the world as they truly find it and find a way to exist in it. In this way, the post-democrat remains open to even more radical possibilities.

Confronting Post-Democracy

To do so, it becomes necessary to cultivate a new form of political subjectivity that not only acknowledges the brute fact of post-democracy, but facilitates a therapeutic engagement with it. In short, a political self-conception oriented toward working through the frustration, anxiety, and alienation inherent in post-democratic life. Over the last decade, no one has made more productive strides in this direction than Jeffrey Green. Though not explicitly engaged with the concept of post-democracy, Green explores and addresses contemporary conditions of political inequality in a way that brilliantly illuminates the greater consequences of these conditions for non-elites. While his earlier work, *The Eyes of The People*, develops a theory of ocular democracy appropriate for a citizenry largely reduced to the role of spectator, his most recent work, *The Shadow of Unfairness*, gives us a broader account of plebeian democracy, one which describes the ubiquitous experience of "second-class citizenship."[44] In particular, Green attends to the more affective repercussions of these conditions, emphasizing how,

> Given the scarcity of political offices and the lack of meaningful forms of active engagement, most citizens find themselves politically unheralded—a condition which, especially in liberal democracies with their official doctrines of equal political influence for the similarly talented and motivated, is likely to be, for many at least, a source of anxiety.[45]

This anxiety, in combination with the indignation and reasonable envy felt toward the wealthy elites who govern, ultimately contributes to discontent; as Green writes, "there can be no expectation of an ordinary citizen's political existence being a happy one."[46]

Thus, Green stresses the need for "ordinary, second-class citizens to find *solace* in the face of the shadow of unfairness"; specifically by, at times, adopting a *"critical indifference* toward active and engaged political life."[47] In other words, individuals should not feel obligated to always participate in politics and should feel comfortable occasionally taking a break. He grounds this indifference on

> an ancient, though largely forgotten, democratic tradition which associates the egalitarian mindset with the tendency to periodically *not to care* about politics — both in the sense of criticizing political life as disrespectful of human equality and, even more, in the sense of celebrating certain practices that draw on political ideals even as these are deployed in a non-political direction.[48]

This tradition, for Green, finds its fullest expression in the work of Epicurus, who taught "that in general a happy life is best secured outside of politics."[49] This is in part due to the distress generated by political activity itself, but also because egalitarian political principles are best realized in the activities and friendships found outside of formal political activity.[50] In other words, at least for the ordinary citizen, a *truly* political life is lived outside of politics, by routinely treating others as equals. Hence, Green's position is not apolitical or antipolitical, but extrapolitical, a way, not of avoiding or preventing politics, but of transcending them.[51]

72 Post-Democratic Political Philosophy

As Green makes clear, however, this indifference is not intended to be permanent, "but only to prevent the discontent likely to characterize their [ordinary citizens'] political lives from extending beyond politics and unduly undermining their overall capacity for well-being and peace of mind."[52] Because, an extrapolitical life is meant to be lived in tandem with a political one, not replace it, the relief Green provides appears oriented toward, not second-class citizens, but political elites.[53] This is further demonstrated by the examples Green employs: those involving Achilles, Otanes (a Persian statesman), and Plato's prototypical democratic.[54] Despite facing setbacks, all are regularly able to exercise a considerable degree of political influence. However, as Green consistently (and rightly) emphasizes, the vast majority of ordinary citizens are not simply disadvantaged, but politically irrelevant; thus, it remains unclear why they would need a way of *momentarily* transcending politics rather than a way of grappling with a *perpetual* exclusion from it.

As such, Green's account, while exemplary in its willingness to reckon with the greater implications of political inequality, does not provide an adequate response to a life of persistent political powerlessness. One could break with Green and imagine ordinary citizens finding some solace by *fully* committing to an extrapolitical life—a private life that seeks to realize political values (e.g., equality) through one's personal relationships, actions, and habits—and adopting a lasting "critical indifference" toward political life properly understood. Yet, by subtly equating extrapolitical power with sovereign power, this would only encourage one to maintain the fantasy of a democratic political existence and avoid actively confronting the real conditions of political powerlessness they face. Given the alternatives, it is perhaps unsurprising that Green ends his book by inviting the reader to have a drink, to "follow Horace when he embraces wine as something 'to bestow fresh hopes, and powerful to wash away the bitterness of care'."[55] Given the state of things, one drink may not be enough.

Unless ordinary citizens are to simply anesthetize themselves, post-democracy requires initiating a conversation about political insignificance in a way that moves beyond treating it simply as a disadvantage or drawback and instead recognizes it as *the* defining feature of one's political existence. To this end, there is no thinker more helpful than Thomas Hobbes. While far from the only philosopher to discuss political powerlessness, Hobbes stands alone in his willingness to inhabit it fully, not in order to critique it as something inferior to a properly political life, but to sketch a robust, edifying account of an alienated political existence on its own terms. Consequently, Chapter Five develops a Hobbesian-inspired model of political subjectivity intended to help the post-democratic citizen work through the frustration, anxiety, and alienation associated with post-democratic life; in short, a therapeutic reading of Hobbes intended for a post-democratic audience.

Notes

1 Aristotle 1998, pp. 1277b–1278a
2 See Dienstag 2006 and Green 2016, ch. 5.
3 Or, as Jason Brennan broadly describes the apathetic or uninformed, "hobbits." See Brennan 2016.
4 Hume [1738] 1994, pp. 51–59
5 Hume [1738] 1994, p. 73
6 Hume [1738] 1994, p. 66
7 Plato 1998, pp. 30a–b
8 See Ure 2008, Sanchez and Stolorow 2013, Crary and Read 2000, and Norris 2017.
9 Peterman 1992, pp. xiii, 29
10 Wittgenstein [1953] 2009, §133
11 In some ways, this is also the aim of democratic realists. Yet, the realist position underestimates the sort of foundational attachments and practices tangled up in this problem, substituting therapeutic work for a public service announcement.
12 Norris 2017, p. 84
13 Cavell [1979] 1999, p. 83
14 Cavell 2013, p. 74
15 Cavell 2013, p. 108
16 Lear 2005, p. 258
17 Peterman 1992, p. 28
18 Glass 1976, p. 181. See Berman 1976.
19 See Deleuze and Guattari 1983 and 1987.
20 Steuernagel 1979, pp. 11–12
21 One can see this shift in Cicero between the call to arms found in *On the Republic* and the resignation of "On Friendship." See Cicero 1923 and Cicero 2009.
22 Seneca 1995, pp. 165–180
23 Tacitus 2009
24 Epictetus 1995, especially § 24 & § 235
25 Foucault 1986, p. 95
26 Foucault 1986, p. 94
27 Lear 2008, p. 2
28 Lear 2008, pp. 48–49
29 Lear 2008, p. 78–79
30 Lear 2008, p. 73
31 Lear 2008, pp. 94–95
32 Dienstag 2006, ch. 1, p. 263
33 Dienstag 2006, p. ix
34 Dienstag 2006, p. 245
35 Dienstag 2006, pp. 256, 264
36 Dienstag 2006, p. 269
37 Dienstag 2006, p. 270
38 Dienstag 2006, pp. xii, 268
39 Dienstag 2006, p. 268
40 Dienstag 2006, p. 268
41 Dienstag 2006, p. 41
42 Dienstag 2006, p. 263
43 Dienstag 2006, p. 248 *italics added*
44 See Green 2009 and Green 2016, ch. 2.
45 Green 2016, p. 135
46 Green 2016, p. 130
47 Green 2016, pp. 11, 131

74 Post-Democratic Political Philosophy

48 Green 2016, p. 131
49 Green 2016, p. 134
50 Green 2016, p. 147
51 Green 2016, p. 131
52 Green 2016, p. 11
53 One can, in fact, imagine former President George W. Bush defending his extended stays at the ranch on such grounds.
54 Green 2016, pp. 150–161
55 Green 2016, p. 164

References

Aristotle. *Politics*. New York: Cambridge UP, 1998.

Berman, Marshall. "Liberal and Totalitarian Therapies in Rousseau: A Response to James M. Glass," *Political Theory* 4. 2 (1976): 185–194.

Brennan, Jason. *Against Democracy*. Princeton, NJ: Princeton UP, 2016.

Cavell, Stanley. *The Claim to Reason*. New York: Oxford UP, [1979] 1999.

Cavell, Stanley. *This New, yet Unapproachable America*. Chicago: University of Chicago Press, 2013.

Cicero. "On Friendship" in *Cicero: On Old Age, On Friendship, On Divination*. Cambridge, MA: Harvard UP, 1923.

Cicero. *The Republic and the Laws*. New York: Oxford UP, 2009.

Crary, Alice and Rupert Read. *The New Wittgenstein*. New York: Routledge Press, 2000.

Deleuze, Gilles and Felix Guattari. *Anti-Oedipus: Capitalism and Schizophrenia*. Minneapolis, MN: University of Minnesota Press, 1983.

Deleuze, Gilles and Felix Guattari. *A Thousand Plateaus: Capitalism and Schizophrenia*. Minneapolis, MN: University of Minnesota Press, 1987.

Dienstag, Joshua Foa. *Pessimism: Philosophy, Ethic, Spirit*. Princeton, NJ: Princeton UP, 2006.

Epictetus. *The Discourses of Epictetus*. New York: Everyman's Library, 1995.

Foucault, Michel. *The History of Sexuality, Vol. 3: The Care of the Self*. New York: Random House, 1986.

Glass, James. "Political Philosophy as Therapy: Rousseau and the Pre-Social Origins of Consciousness," *Political Theory* 4. 2(1976): 163–184.

Green, Jeffrey. *The Eyes of the People: Democracy in an Age of Spectatorship*. New York: Oxford UP, 2009.

Green, Jeffrey. *The Shadow of Unfairness: A Plebeian Theory of Liberal Democracy*. New York: Oxford UP, 2016.

Hume, David. "A Treatise of Human Nature" in *Political Writings*. Stuart Warner and Donald Livingston, eds. Indianapolis, IN: Hackett Publishing, [1738] 1994.

Lear, Jonathan. *Freud*. New York: Routledge Press, 2005.

Lear, Jonathan. *Radical Hope: Ethics in the Face of Cultural Devastation*. Cambridge, MA: Harvard UP, 2008.

Norris, Andrew. *Becoming Who We Are*. New York: Oxford UP, 2017.

Peterman, James. *Philosophy as Therapy*. Albany, NY: State University of New York Press, 1992.

Plato. "Apology" in *Four Texts on Socrates: Plato's Euthyphro, Apology, and Crito and Aristophanes' Clouds*. Thomas G. West and Grace Starry West, eds. Ithaca, NY: Cornell UP, 1998.

Sanchez, Robert E. and Robert D. Stolorow. "Psyches Therapeia: Therapeutic Dimensions in Heidegger and Wittgenstein," *Comparative and Continental Philosophy* 5. 1 (2003): 67–80.

Seneca. "On the Private Life" in *Moral and Political Essays*. John M. Cooper and J. F. Procopé, eds. New York: Cambridge UP, 1995.

Steuernagel, Gertrude. *Political Philosophy as Therapy: Marcuse Reconsidered*. Westport, CT: Greenwood Press, 1979.

Tacitus. *Agricola and Germany*. New York: Oxford UP, 2009.

Ure, Michael. *Nietzsche's Therapy: Self Cultivation in the Middle Works*. Lanham, MD: Lexington Books, 2008.

Wittgenstein, Ludwig. *Philosophical Investigations*. Malden, MA: Blackwell Publishing, [1953] 2009.

5

POST-DEMOCRATIC CITIZENSHIP

In Chapter Four, we examined the way in which a post-democratic diagnosis invites a *therapeutic* approach to political philosophy, one which breaks with the *practico-political* approach fostered by democratic theory. Instead of treating political philosophy as a means of developing and refining the citizen's political judgment, a therapeutic approach is intended to help individuals alleviate the frustration, anxiety, and alienation that stem from post-democratic life; in particular, the experience of political domination. But what would such an approach look like? This chapter offers a therapeutic reading of the work of Thomas Hobbes, specifically his account of servitude, as a means of demonstrating both the mode of political philosophy appropriate to post-democracy and further elaborating the conditions of post-democratic citizenship. In doing so, it provides a model of citizenship that can serve as a foundation for grappling with and, ideally, working through an awareness of one's own political powerlessness.

After first illustrating how post-democracy constitutes a species of political domination, I will introduce Hobbes's account of servitude by way of contrasting it with his account of subjecthood. In doing so, I will show how the Hobbesian subject's self-understanding encourages an unfounded optimism toward sovereignty—one which mirrors the democratic citizen's own—while the servant's self-understanding better prepares contemporary citizens for an explicit and, hence, productive engagement with the more distressing consequences of post-democratic sovereignty. I will then explore how the servant's perspective can inform a post-democratic political logic that addresses questions of legitimacy, membership, responsibility, and culpability. I will end by stressing the need for a practical realization of one's post-democratic identity as part of the therapeutic process, one which I will further elaborate in Chapter Six.

Post-Democratic Political Domination

What does it mean to be dominated? Drawing upon both Max Weber and William Connolly, Philip Pettit explains that "One agent dominates another if and only if they have a certain power over that other, in particular power of interference on an arbitrary basis."[1] In order to suggest that post-democratic citizens should consider themselves dominated by the state, it is necessary to show that the state constitutes an agent with the power to interfere with them on an arbitrary basis. To be an agent, Pettit explains, the entity must be able to act intentionally; agents of domination "cannot just be a system or network or whatever," but must either "be a personal or corporate or collective agent."[2] Understanding the state as a series of interrelated institutions, it clearly has the potential to function as both a corporate and collective agent with the capability to dominate others. A post-democratic outlook further allows us to interpret the state as beholden to various elite interests, even if they are, at times, in conflict with one another.

While the state's capacity to interfere with its citizens is self-evident, the idea that it acts on an arbitrary basis when doing so demands further demonstration. As Pettit explains,

> What is required for non-arbitrary state power … is that the power be exercised in a way that tracks, not the power-holder's personal welfare or world-view, but rather the welfare and world-view of the public. The acts of interference perpetrated by the state must be triggered by the shared interests of those affected under an interpretation of what those interests require that is shared, at least at the procedural level, by those affected.[3]

In other words, a sovereign power acts arbitrarily when it ignores the collective needs and beliefs of those it governs. It could be argued that, even when political power is largely a matter of elite competition, elected officials, by design, must appeal to the interests and opinions of their constituencies, and thus necessarily track "the welfare and world-view of the public."

Yet, this assumes, first, that these elected officials are responsive to the *actual* concerns of their constituencies, as opposed to engaging in fear-mongering; second, that the interests or ideas championed are not "sectional or factional in character," or worse, simply intended to exploit their constituency's divisiveness over minor issues; and, third, that these interests and ideas eventually play a role in influencing sovereign decision-making instead of merely remaining empty rhetoric.[4] Under post-democratic conditions, these are hardly unproblematic assumptions. Moreover, for those committed to a more substantive level of democratic participation, it is not enough for sovereign power to instrumentally track the public's interests for the purposes of re-election; rather, the state must act as an extension of an active public. Otherwise, it would be disingenuous to

78 Post-Democratic Citizenship

characterize sovereign decision-making as being triggered by a *shared* interpretation of what those interests require (i.e., consideration through a democratic practice), instead of simply a series of periodic opportunities for elite competition.

Yet, Pettit does emphasize that the question of political domination, though a matter of interpretation, is not *"essentially* value-laden."[5] Rather,

> the identification of a certain sort of state action as arbitrary and dominating is an essentially political matter; it is not something on which theorists can decide in the calmness of their studies ... what has to be established is whether people really are dominated, not whether domination is visible from within some privileged evaluative standpoint. As the facts of the matter, including facts about local culture and context, determine whether a certain act counts as interference, so the facts of the matter determine whether a certain act of interference counts as arbitrary.[6]

Thus, the question of domination cannot be decided from a third-person perspective, but only by those actually experiencing the interference in question. This consideration is further troubled by the observation, expounded upon in Chapter Two, that most individuals living under post-democratic conditions either do not recognize their political practices as insufficiently democratic or, if they do, maintain the belief that such malfunctions are only temporary or irregular. Obviously, if most citizens believe that the state is democratic enough, then even if they are demonstrably misinformed or uninterested in an accurate characterization of their relationship with sovereignty, they will not experience post-democratic sovereignty as a form of domination, much in the same way those who refuse to accept the idea that smoking is dangerous will not think about the act of smoking as a form of self-harm.

Yet, to the extent that the democratic values of popular sovereignty and political equality are considered important—as they tend to be in political contexts so accustomed to democratic concepts and language—*and* the individual cares enough to investigate whether these values are being realized through political practice, post-democratic sovereignty would certainly appear as a form of domination. Even if, through embracing democratic realism, one were to assume that all of the value placed on popular sovereignty and political equality is 'just talk,' granting a measure of cognitive dissonance that would allow most to feel as if they were not dominated, such an arrangement would still constitute an experience of domination for those at all still sympathetic toward democratic principles. One may further argue that a democratic citizenry can never truly be dominated, that they always have the ability to rebel or "exit" by leaving or simply ignoring the state.[7] A post-democratic diagnosis does not exclude such possibilities, but it does consider them extremely unlikely, exceptions to a daily political reality that remains primarily marked by domination.

Still, it is important to note that just because post-democratic sovereignty acts arbitrarily does not mean it will not occasionally or even regularly act in a manner consistent with one's interests. In other words, the fact that one is dominated hardly means that one will find fault with the way in which sovereign power interferes in their lives; one may even find greater fault in the state's unwillingness to interfere further (e.g., by not passing laws to prevent other, non-governmental forms of domination). As such, domination should not be thought of as necessarily leading to political dissatisfaction, or at least not total dissatisfaction, but only as the *de facto* inability to influence how one is governed. What remains essential for a post-democratic outlook is that the alignment of one's personal preferences with elite interests is seen as neither causal nor correlative, but coincidental, making it both contingent and unpredictable.[8]

To all but the most committed authoritarians, it would be odd not to find post-democratic domination, at the very least, undesirable. Still, just as one does not deal with an illness by ignoring it, an aversion to domination should not keep the post-democratic citizens from considering how it structures their relationship with sovereignty and with each other. To develop a more robust picture of the experience of post-democratic sovereignty, we now turn to a thinker not often associated with democratic theory, but the philosophical underpinnings of modern political domination: Thomas Hobbes.

Hobbesian Inroads into Post-Democratic Philosophy

Despite the fact that he describes sovereignty as an absolute right to dominion, some may have reservations with treating Hobbes as a theorist of domination, particularly because Hobbes's account of subjecthood breaks so decisively with Pettit's emphasis on arbitrary interference.[9] As even the most casual readers of Hobbes are aware, subjects come together to form a covenant to authorize the sovereign's absolute power "for their peace and common defence."[10] This follows from Hobbes's argument that sovereign power is only effective when it is both overwhelming and unrestricted, able to make use of all of the commonwealth's resources, including its inhabitants, as it sees fit; anything less would inhibit the sovereign's ability to protect individuals against a violent, untimely death, undermining the ostensible purpose of the commonwealth in the first place. To the extent that the sovereign intentionally and exclusively pursues this aim, sovereign authority would not be experienced as a form of domination, but rather as a kind of mediated autonomy in which the sovereign non-arbitrarily tracks the "welfare and world-view" of those governed by ensuring their safety and security. For this reason, the Hobbesian subject constitutes a less-than-perfect model for post-democratic citizenship.

Yet, readers of Hobbes are often quick to forget that he offers not one, but two distinct models of political subjectivity.[11] Across his three major works of systematic political thought—*The Elements of the Law, On the Citizen,* and *Leviathan*—Hobbes

80 Post-Democratic Citizenship

consistently differentiates between the *subject* and the *servant*. While the former democratically institutes an artificial commonwealth with other subjects, forming a covenant "of every man with every man," the servant joins the natural common-wealth when conquered by another, specifically by covenanting directly with the sovereign as to "avoid the present stroke of death," by offering in exchange "that so long as his life and the liberty of his body is allowed him, the victor shall have the use thereof, at his pleasure."[12] Despite scholars typically being quick to privilege the former, anyone with a basic awareness of world history would be well aware that most states are founded on the basis of violence, not universal consent. As Hume explains,

> Were you to preach, in most parts of the world, that political connexions are found altogether on voluntary consent or a mutual promise, the magistrate would soon imprison you, as seditious, for loosening the ties of obedience; if your friends did not before shut you up as delirious, for advancing such absurdities ... Almost all the governments, which exist at present, or of which there remains any record in story, have been founded originally, either on usurpation or conquest, or both, without any pretense of a fair consent or voluntary subjection of people.[13]

By describing the commonwealth born of violence as "natural," Hobbes can reasonably be interpreted as having a similar view. Thus, despite the often exclusive attention given to the subject, Hobbes's readership seems to be primarily made up of servants.

Additionally, Hobbes's account of servitude offers a model of citizenship that more readily fits with Pettit's understanding of domination as a form of arbitrary interference.[14] Though the servant covenants with the sovereign as well, technically authorizing all future exercises of sovereign power, the conditions under which this occurs radically distinguishes the servant from the subject by illuminating the flimsy, if not wholly imaginary, connection between sovereign authority and the servant's "welfare and world-view." Because the servant covenants only to avoid the immediate threat of death or imprisonment, the sovereign's authority rests, not on the servant's ongoing interest in security (as it does for the subject), but the servant's desire to avoid a loss of life or freedom *in one particular instance*. Future sovereign decisions, which may have nothing at all to do with the servant's well-being (much less world-view), would only be seen as non-arbitrary because the servant, at one time, had no other choice but to submit. Unless we are similarly willing to recognize the rightful authority of the kidnapper or other violent criminals, it is difficult to classify servitude as anything other than domination.

Furthermore, in equating the servant and subject in terms of political status, Hobbes illuminates the extent to which the subject's awareness of domination is a function of belief rather than actual sovereign decision-making; in short, it is not

Post-Democratic Citizenship **81**

a matter of *how* the sovereign interferes, but of the way in which the non-sovereign individual *interprets* that interference. If, for instance, the subject no longer recognizes the sovereign's actions as being in the service of the subject's safety and security, then regardless of the covenant made, the subject would experience the sovereign's authority as a form of domination. As David Gauthier points out,

> If we regard the subject similarly [to the servant] … then Hobbes's account begins to assume a totalitarian dimension … Indeed he invites the rejoinder, urged strongly by Locke, that the sovereign is the enemy of the subjects, and an enemy given the strength to overpower and destroy them by their own act in creating him.[15]

What, then, ultimately distinguishes subject from servant is the former's faith that this is simply not the case, while the latter never had any reason to imagine that it would be otherwise.

These competing interpretations of sovereign authority thus lead the servant and subject to develop two distinct dispositions toward political authority and activity. In a nutshell, though the Hobbesian subjects' participation in the founding allows them to imagine themselves as the authors of their own domination, treating the commonwealth as an instrument in the service of their self-preservation, the servant operates under no such illusions. Having been forcibly incorporated into the commonwealth, the servant is unable to recognize the sovereign's domination as either an extension of their will or necessarily being in their best interest, except, of course, their immediate interest in avoiding death or imprisonment. This leads the servant to adopt a set of inferences that are fundamentally distinct from those held by the Hobbesian subject; in particular, while the latter holds that the individual's relationship to sovereignty is intentional, shared, mediated by community, and guaranteed by consent, the former considers it accidental, solitary, unmediated, and guaranteed by violence. As such, while the Hobbesian subject exhibits a fundamentally hopeful disposition vis-a-vis political activity and authority, the Hobbesian servant's disposition is primarily informed by an underlying fear of sovereign power. Insofar as Hobbes emphasizes that "the rights and consequences of sovereignty are the same in both [commonwealths]," this should lead us to be wary of embracing the subject's hopeful disposition when unable to share their faith concerning the sovereign's intentions.[16]

In this sense, the relationship between the Hobbesian servant and subject mirrors the contrast between the self-understood democratic citizen and post-democratic citizen, respectively, under post-democratic conditions. Whereas the democratic citizen maintains the belief or fantasy that political practices continue to satisfy or, at least, approximate democratic criteria, the post-democratic citizen recognizes their inability to realize either popular sovereignty or political equality. As such, Hobbes's account of servitude not only provides a model of citizenship

82 Post-Democratic Citizenship

better able to inform an understanding of post-democratic political life, but further illustrates the way it productively departs from an overly stubborn democratic outlook on politics. In other words, their shared awareness of domination gives post-democratic citizens good reason to discard the fantasy of a sovereign power either responsive to their preferences or invested in their well-being, instead favoring a sober confrontation with the bleak realities of post-democratic life. After further developing this claim by diving deeper into the dispositional implications of Hobbes's competing models of citizenship, this chapter will conclude by showing the way in which an account of Hobbesian servitude can inform a distinctly post-democratic approach to questions of legitimacy, membership, responsibility, and culpability.

The Subject and the Servant

How, then, does the servant's political self-understanding lead to a different disposition toward sovereign power from that of the subject? What first distinguishes the servant from the subject is the degree to which they each consciously decide to join the commonwealth. For the subject or, rather, subject-to-be, the formation of the commonwealth follows from their realization that a life well lived is impossible under an indefinite state of war, which only offers the "continual fear and danger of violent death" and an existence famously described as "solitary, poor, nasty, brutish, and short."[17] In order to escape these miserable conditions, the subject gathers their neighbors and convinces them that their only hope for security lies in their willingness to collectively give up their natural rights and agree to submit to a single sovereign power, who "may use the strength and means of them all, as he shall think expedient, for their peace and common defence."[18] The artificial commonwealth thus appears as a novel, self-generated solution to the threats posed by an anarchic world.

For the servant, however, the natural commonwealth results, not from a conscious effort on their part, but from the servant's abduction by another. After being taken prisoner, the servant's captor offers to spare the servant's life and allow them to keep their corporeal liberty on the condition that they recognize the captor's absolute authority over them, explicitly promising to obey all commands and "not to run away, nor do violence" to their newfound master.[19] If the servant refuses, their captor may either kill or imprison them, reducing them, in Hobbes's technical sense of the term, to a slave.[20] Thus, whereas the subject's choice to join the commonwealth is intentional, the servant's is accidental, contingent upon both their capture and the subsequent opportunity given to remain both free and alive. As such, the natural commonwealth presents itself, not as the resolution of a perennial problem, but as the best possible outcome following a series of unfortunate events.[21]

Overall, this contributes to quite a different perspective on the servant's relationship to sovereignty. In not being the product of design, but something forced upon the servant, the commonwealth will always be an alien institution; though the servant belongs to it, the commonwealth is not theirs. As a result, the servant remains acutely aware that their contribution to the commonwealth is inessential, that its existence is distinct from their own. Additionally, the servant is consistently reminded that, had they only evaded capture, their situation could have been different. For the Hobbesian subject, there is always the possibility that they could have decided to remain under a state of war, but the fact that they actively chose to form the artificial commonwealth would seem to paint the outcome as a logical, if not an inevitable one. The natural commonwealth, rather, takes the form of an aberration, a product, not of ingenuity or destiny, but of a misstep. In light of these considerations, the servant considers the sovereign neither necessary nor as an extension of their will, but as an extrinsic, inescapable burden that they have no choice but to obey.

The servant's experience of domination is further differentiated from that of the Hobbesian subject in that it is solitary, depriving them of a greater political community. In contrast, the subject forms a multilateral covenant with all other subjects, and while this is hardly the sort of political friendships celebrated in Aristotle and Cicero, these covenants not only facilitated the past exercise of political influence (i.e., in naming the sovereign), but serve as a persistent reminder that the covenanters are both collectively responsible for the commonwealth and directly responsible to one another. They are, politically speaking, in it together. As such, the subject can look to other subjects and recognize a shared commitment, one which not only binds them in a way distinct from the relationship they may share as friends or even fellow human beings, but also one to which they can appeal when holding one another accountable for both maintaining the commonwealth and obeying sovereign commands. For instance, the subject should feel justified in requiring her fellow subjects to enlist in military service or to chastise them for breaking the law; their failure to do so constitutes, not the violation of an abstract obligation to the state, but a disregard for the explicit agreement made with their fellow subjects. Even when the commonwealth is dissolving, there must be a *collective* recognition of the sovereign's failure to protect them.

The servant, however, never makes a pact with other servants. Upon capture, the servant covenants exclusively with the sovereign, leaving them politically isolated. This is not to say, of course, that the servant remains completely alone; we would fully expect them to interact socially, economically, and so on, with others. Yet, in neither being preceded by nor aspiring to the exercise of influence over sovereign decision-making, these relationships would be inherently apolitical. In contrast to the covenant the subject shares with his fellow subjects, the servant can only look to other servants as having made a commitment similar to their own. They are not responsible to each other, but only to the sovereign, and subsequently they can distinguish between crimes against the commonwealth and crimes against one another. In other words, the servant's decision to cheat on

84 Post-Democratic Citizenship

their taxes or avoid military service is not necessarily anyone else's concern; another servant may still call upon the sovereign to dispense justice, but this follows from that servant's allegiance to the commonwealth, not any direct claim the servant has against the initial offender. All of this makes it unclear whether servants can even properly be described as being united rather than merely lumped together. Their parallel experiences might lead to a greater affinity for one another, a sort of 'imagined community' in Benedict Anderson's sense, but without the immediate political relationships to one another that distinguish the artificial commonwealth, all servants share politically is their obedience to a common sovereign.[22]

In addition to depriving the servant of a greater political community, the servant's direct covenant with the sovereign renders their relationship unmediated. This again stands in contrast with the subject who, at least initially, does not engage with the sovereign at all; the subject only comes to recognize sovereign power through the covenant they make with their fellow subjects, which, in turn, mediates their relationship to sovereignty as a whole. As a result, the artificial commonwealth takes on the appearance, not of sovereign power, but of the political community that instituted it. Nowhere is this more evident than the frontispiece which adorns the 1651 edition of *Leviathan*, which famously depicts the sovereign as constituted by "the multitude so united."[23] This metaphor both reflects and helps cultivate the sense that the commonwealth is, at its core, the unity of its members, encouraging the subject to recognize it as an extension of a collective will shared with their neighbors. By overlaying this image of a constitutive community of subjects over the absolute authority exercised by sovereign power, the artificial commonwealth is able to more easily facilitate the subject's identification with it.

The natural commonwealth, however, fails to take on the identity of a greater political community precisely because, for the servant, that community never existed. Instead, the servant's solitary, violent subjugation leads them to interpret the commonwealth as an expression, not of a collective desire for peace and security, but of sovereign might. Without the image of a political community to mediate the servant's relationship with sovereignty, the state appears simply as the sovereign institutions that govern the servant; for example the police, military, administrative bureaucracies, and so on. As such, the sovereign is less able to masquerade as an extension of the community which, at least on the subject's account, it is intended to serve, allowing the servant to more easily distinguish the actions and interests of sovereign power from their own. Just as the accidental quality of their relationship to sovereignty encourages the servant to see it as something alien, the inability to substitute a representation of one's community for the commonwealth itself further cements the idea that it is something distinct from not only them, but their neighbors as well. As such, the constitutive relationship suggested by *Leviathan's* frontispiece would seem deeply misleading. From the servant's perspective, the more likely interpretation would not be that sovereign power originates from the commonwealth's inhabitants, but that the sovereign, like the giant Polyphemus that terrorized Odysseus and his crew, has merely consumed them. In this sense, the sovereign would appear much closer to the monstrous sea creature from which Hobbes takes the name 'Leviathan' in the first place.

Finally, the servant accepts that their relationship with sovereignty is both founded and sustained principally by the sovereign's threat of and capacity for violence. The subject, while recognizing this aspect of sovereignty as well, does so to a lesser degree, instead framing the subject's experience of domination as one to which she has deliberately consented. Some may still wish to take the hard-line Hobbesian position and argue that, because both commonwealths are founded, in the last instance, upon covenants, the natural commonwealth is just as much grounded upon consent as the artificial commonwealth. Yet, such a position would fail to recognize how the contextual differences between the two would color the covenants made. Having actively willed the artificial commonwealth into existence, the subject can treat the possibility of sovereign violence as a distant one, perhaps imperative for holding others to their word, but ultimately unnecessary for guaranteeing their obedience. Moreover, without any prior exposure to sovereign violence, the subject may be able to remain comfortably unaware that violence could ever actually be used against them. Like the pollyannaish individual shocked by the state's indiscriminate or unwarranted use of force, the thought may never have even occurred to them.

The servant has no such luxury. Sovereign violence is not tangential to their relationship to the commonwealth, but a precondition for it, making it difficult to ever disassociate the two. The natural commonwealth, in other words, can never shake the connotation made explicit by its other title: the commonwealth by acquisition.[24] As such, the sovereign no longer appears as an entrusted guardian, but, much like the mafioso offering 'protection,' as paradoxically both the greatest threat to the servant's well-being and the only means of their self-preservation. This, in turn, renders the servant's consent a secondary consideration, itself derived from their initial experience of 'being acquired,' leaving the act of consent, not a signal of the servant's investment in the commonwealth, but solely an expedient way of avoiding further imprisonment or death. Thus, for the servant, the fact that they have consented hardly seems to matter; what primarily shapes their perception of the commonwealth is the persistent, underlying possibility of enduring sovereign violence once more.

Democratic Hope and Post-Democratic Fear

Though their contrasting experiences would lead us to assume that the Hobbesian subject and servant would have radically different dispositions toward sovereignty, Hobbes, by the time he writes *Leviathan*, attempts to show that the two are actually more similar than we would otherwise expect. Despite all of their differences, he argues, they are both motivated by fear. Of the natural commonwealth, he writes,

86 Post-Democratic Citizenship

> this kind of dominion or sovereignty differeth from sovereignty by institution only in this, that men who choose their sovereign do so for fear of one another, and not of him whom they institute; but in this case they subject themselves to him they are afraid of. In both cases, they do it for fear.[25]

Leo Strauss offers an explanation as to why Hobbes may have been so invested in joining these seemingly disparate experiences together. Specifically, he interprets this move of Hobbes's as a part of his effort to "more systematically" reconcile "the involuntary as well as voluntary nature of subjection" for the purposes of silencing his democratic critics, who would inevitably favor the artificial commonwealth.[26] In order "to show that democracy can do nothing better than transform itself into an absolute monarchy ... he sought a common motive for the founding of the artificial as well as of the natural State," one which he found "in the fear of violent death, which had originally, as it seems, connected only with the natural State."[27] In short, if both commonwealths are the products of fear, there is no reason to prefer a democratic founding to a coercive one.

However, this exclusive emphasis on fear represents a substantive break with his earlier characterization of the two commonwealths. Previously, Strauss explains, his openness toward democratic ideas led him to more definitely distinguish between the two, maintaining that "the motive which leads to the natural State is fear" while "the motive that leads to the artificial State is hope or trust."[28] This distinction is most apparent in his first systematic work of political philosophy, *The Elements of the Law*, where he explains that,

> he that subjecteth himself uncompelled, thinketh there is good reason he should be better used, than he that doth it upon compulsion; and coming in freely, calleth himself, though in subjection, a FREEMAN; whereby it appeareth that liberty is not any exemption from subjection and obedience to the sovereign power, but a state of better hope than theirs, that have been subjected by force or conquest.[29]

Such a description, at odds with Hobbes's later account, seems much more in line with what we would expect from the subject and servant's respective entries into the commonwealth. Though the subject's decision to found the artificial commonwealth does rest upon a fear of others, the commonwealth itself represents a beacon of hope, a chance to extinguish that fear by placing one's faith in a sovereign power capable of guaranteeing protection. The servant may have similar fears, but the natural commonwealth appears, not as means of overcoming them, but as their realization; it is, short of a violent death, the servant's worst nightmare come to fruition. As such, there seems to be good reason to qualitatively distinguish the particular fears which motivate each party—to separate the subject's *hypothetical* fear of a third party from the servant's *extant* fear of sovereign

Post-Democratic Citizenship **87**

power itself—and side with the early Hobbes, who distinguished between the two on the basis of hope and fear.

Moreover, this dispositive distinction proves crucial for demonstrating how a post-democratic outlook departs from its democratic counterpart. Overall, the model of Hobbesian subjecthood exemplifies how a democratic perspective can fundamentally mystify the experience of domination by encouraging subjects to see themselves as its authors and, subsequently, think of sovereign power as acting in their best interest, even without the ability to exercise any real influence over sovereign decision-making. Transfixed by an initial democratic moment (i.e., the founding), subjects cling to the idea that they still somehow have some latent or tenuous control over their situation, giving them reason to be hopeful. Subjects see the state as an extension of themselves, representative of a greater political community to which they belong and owing its very existence to their willingness to acknowledge its authority. In this sense, the democratic narrative that distinguishes them from the servant leaves subjects convinced that, despite all evidence to the contrary, the commonwealth is beholden to them, as if their experience of domination is a mere formality necessary to satisfy the logic of sovereignty but in no way reflective of the facts on the ground.

The servant, like the self-aware post-democratic citizen, knows better. Based on a particular understanding of their relationship to sovereign power, the servant is able to recognize that the Hobbesian subject's hope, like that of the self-understood democratic citizen living under post-democratic conditions, lacks any and all foundation. Whether natural or artificial, the commonwealth is in no way obligated to the non-sovereign individual; though the sovereign may have a vested interest in their protection, both the level and character of this protection is decided exclusively by the sovereign.[30] As such, the subject and servant's shared experience of domination neither has any substantive connection to their consent—deliberate or otherwise—nor any necessary relation to their preferences, whether understood more broadly (i.e., as they pertain to policy) or solely in terms of their personal security. Rather, it is simply a function of their inability to contest it. As it turns out, the essential difference between the two models of political subjectivity is not that the subject has real reason to hope; instead, as Hobbes himself makes clear, it is that the subject confidently builds their own cage, while the servant finds one ready-made. Thus, the early Hobbes, when juxtaposed with his later writings, gives us insight into not only how the subject and servant differ in terms of their political dispositions, but also why the subject's hopeful self-conception ultimately contributes to an illusory understanding of their relationship with sovereignty, one which attempts to veil their domination with a thin cloak of self-determination.

It is precisely for this reason that the post-democratic citizen must take pains to break with a democratic model of citizenship. The democratic citizen, like the Hobbesian subject, is predisposed to think about their relationship to sovereignty in light of their active role in creating it; while the Hobbesian subject focuses

88 Post-Democratic Citizenship

exclusively on their participation in the founding, democratic citizens see themselves as consistently exercising influence over sovereign decision-making through both formal and informal means. Under post-democratic conditions, however, this is a mistake. What Hobbes's account of the subject shows is that, even when an individual is explicitly aware of being dominated, the belief that they have an active role to play can muddle this awareness to the point that the individual becomes unable to draw the appropriate conclusions from it. In short, that the self-understood democratic citizen's token participation overshadows their real, non-democratic subjugation.

A Post-Democratic Political Logic

In order, therefore, to avoid the trappings of a democratic mythos, however subtle, the post-democratic citizen should try to think like a Hobbesian servant. Specifically, this involves avoiding the impulse to imagine one's membership in the commonwealth as either deliberate or intentional, one's relationship to other citizens as politically relevant, or sovereign power as either representative of or indebted to the greater community in which one lives, and instead internalizing the realization that one has only an accidental, solitary relationship with a sovereign power both alien and violent. Above all else, it is to recognize that one has no real say over one's own domination by a sovereign power, consistently troubling any hope one might have had over its exercise.[31] This is not to imply that one must always be afraid, ceaselessly anxious over the state's capacity for violence (though some historical targets of state violence have good reason to be), but that the state should always be feared as one would fear any other sort of unpredictable externality—such as a foreign occupation, a natural disaster, a plague, or divine intervention—able to severely disrupt or prematurely end one's life. Beyond contributing a generally pessimistic outlook on sovereign power, what exactly are the greater implications of recognizing the experience of domination as central for post-democratic citizenship? Insofar as it provides an instructive model of domination, how can an account of Hobbesian servitude help inform a post-democratic approach to questions of legitimacy, membership, responsibility, and culpability?

To begin, the manner in which the servant consents to sovereign power leads us to believe that consent is more a matter of self-preservation than a judicious acknowledgment of the sovereign's legitimate authority; the servant agrees to recognize the sovereign *as* sovereign, not because of any of the sovereign's merits, but because the sovereign has a knife to their throat. Yet, for Hobbes, sovereign legitimacy depends exclusively on whether this consent has been obtained.[32] This leaves us with two options: to either consider the servant's consent as inherently significant, despite the fact that it is given under duress, and thus preserve legitimacy's import, or to recognize the state's claim to legitimacy as essentially hollow, as demonstrating no more than the state's capacity to coerce. While Hobbes no doubt sought to convince us of the former by prioritizing his account of the subject's consent (which could conceivably ground the legitimacy of the sovereign), the fact that he ultimately equates the subject's consent with that of the servant should give us pause. Rather, his understanding of consent, at least in the servant's case, seems to paint legitimacy solely as indicative of the servant's desire to remain both free and alive.

Overall, the greater lesson seems to be that a more meaningful understanding of legitimacy (i.e., as an indicator of the sovereign's *right* to govern) has no place in a political context primarily defined by the experience of domination. In other words, legitimacy claims that appeal to something other than the state's overwhelming capacity for violence are politically inconsequential. This is not to say that such claims are, in themselves, insignificant or meaningless; the act of judging the state's legitimacy still allows individuals to clarify, at least to themselves, what they consider to be important criteria for evaluating the state as well as how they feel about the state as a whole. Yet, whereas illegitimacy prompts the democratic citizen to engage in political activity, the post-democratic citizen, aware of the severe limitations of their political agency, no longer treats the state's illegitimacy as an invitation to act. Unlike an authentically Hobbesian authoritarianism, however, a post-democratic context affords the individual opportunities to "act." Still, like the servant, the post-democratic citizen finds themself in a position where efficacious political participation is individually costly and statistically improbable. Thus, it does not seem to matter whether the state is legitimate or not; all that matters is whether the state is powerful enough to continue to ensure their domination.

Moreover, the inability to hold sovereign power accountable to a higher standard of legitimacy troubles the idea that the post-democratic citizen can expect anything from the state at all. For instance, we could imagine a post-democratic citizen thinking, "though the state seems to be indefensibly illegitimate, at least I can count on the state to acknowledge my legal standing, maintain a growing economy, or protect me from a violent death." Yet, lacking in political agency, the post-democratic citizen is left without any sort of guarantee that the state will continue to satisfy these sorts of expectations. At some point, whether through threat of violence or loss of steam, the direct action considered democracy's failsafe will slow, and the formal mechanisms meant to correct the ship will only serve to circumscribe political possibility and confirm the post-democratic citizen's sense of their own political impotence. The only reliable indicator of what can be expected depends upon the level of elite consensus the issue satisfies; how long any idea or policy can maintain that position remains an empirical question. At present (and thankfully), widespread legal personhood, economic growth, and peace seem to enjoy this status. Still, all the post-democratic citizen can truly expect from the state—whether directed by economic elites, populist demagogues, or a revolving door of factions all self-identifying as the *demos*—is that it will do all in its power to maintain its sovereignty. All else remains speculation.

90 Post-Democratic Citizenship

Whereas the experience of domination diminishes the significance of legitimacy by rendering it moot, it effects a dramatic shift in the way in which the post-democratic citizen conceptualizes their membership in the body politic. Under a democratic framework, membership is a question of participation; one is a member to the extent that one possesses the opportunity to influence sovereign decision-making. A post-democratic framework, however, transforms the question of membership into one of subjugation; one is a member to the extent that one consents to being dominated.[33] Yet, in contrast with the Hobbesian subject, this consent does not signal the post-democratic citizen's active affirmation of the state. Rather, like the servant, it reflects the conditions of domination the post-democratic citizen always-already endures, an artifact, not of their faith in sovereign power, but of their desire to avoid imprisonment or death.

This would seem to imply that post-democratic membership is entirely a passive experience, simply involving one's submission to the state. At least politically, it does. Ultimately, this submission allows the post-democratic citizen to more effectively navigate the complex socio-economic environment both fostered and contained by the exercise of sovereign power. According to Pettit, being dominated does not preclude the ability to make decisions; rather, all it highlights is the inability to contest the power of others to arbitrarily interfere with the decision-making process. As we tend to see in contemporary post-democratic political contexts, not all choices are determined for the non-sovereign individual in advance. If anything, the sort of economic policies that continue to sustain wealth disparities seem to depend on a form of domination far from total, instead allowing the post-democratic citizen a wide range of choices. These would still be dominated choices, as elite preferences can still direct the state to interfere with them on an arbitrary basis, but they would be, at least in the immediate sense, un-coerced, hypothetically giving the post-democratic citizen the opportunity to act in their own interest.

As such, the post-democratic citizen is not a slave (in Hobbes's sense of the term), bound in chains and unable to make any decisions. Though they have no control over their political environment, they are still able to act within that environment, as well as exploit its particular features. The post-democratic citizen can, in other words, still 'tend to their own garden', despite having to adhere to the limits placed upon it (and them) by the state. For instance, Hobbes stresses that, though subjects and servants do not have an absolute right to property—they must relinquish it when ordered to do so by the sovereign power—they can still exercise property rights in relation to other non-sovereign individuals.[34] Similarly, the post-democratic citizen, despite being dominated by the state, can still make use of aspects of their domination, not in a way that subverts or resists the overall domination they experience, but in order to make the best of their situation.

Thus, while post-democratic membership might initially appear to solely be a cause for resignation, it also invites the post-democratic citizen to embrace a purely instrumental understanding of their relationship with sovereignty. The state, rather than taking the form of a collective project, exists only as a tool wielded by those able to exercise political influence; for those lacking such influence, the state constitutes a set of externally imposed conditions. In contrast with some variants of liberalism, most notably Rawls's own, this instrumental approach to sovereignty relieves the post-democratic citizen of the mistaken notion that the state constitutes a means by which they can realize their autonomy.[35] By purging themselves of any sort of existential identification with the state, the post-democratic citizens remain better able to appreciate the state as something alien to them, consequently better preparing them to anticipate its fundamental unpredictability as well as lack of regard for either their preferences or well-being.

Though unable to decide upon these conditions themselves, post-democratic citizens can nevertheless attempt to make use of the conditions in order to realize their own ends. This is not to suggest that the state will not, at times, frustrate the post-democratic citizen's ability to decide on personally significant private matters. Depending on the significance and repercussions of those foreclosed decisions, the state can certainly create situations that may prove unbearable. Still, the hope remains that other conditions will either serve to facilitate the individual's ability to pursue their interests or will be exploitable enough, by means of a technicality or novel interpretation, to do so all the same. Of course, as these conditions will inevitably shift, the post-democratic citizen must further be ready to consistently adapt themself accordingly. As such, they find themselves playing a perpetual game of Frogger, ceaselessly dodging oncoming hazards while, in lieu of ever escaping them, searching for brief intervals of peace.

The post-democratic citizen's responsibility to sovereign power follows from this logic of instrumentality. While a democratic political logic presupposes that the individual's responsibility stems from their status as a participant, a post-democratic logic recognizes a responsibility to the state solely on the basis of the individual's interest in preserving their life and freedom. In other words, they need only obey the law and/or serve the state (e.g., by enlisting in military service, reporting on the crimes of others, serving on a jury, etc.) to the extent that they consider doing so necessary to either prevent the state's collapse or avoid running afoul of sovereign power. They may still decide to follow the law or engage in service out of certain ethical convictions, but, in such cases, the post-democratic citizen is only coincidentally satisfying any sort of presumed political responsibility. In other words, they may refrain from murder, but not because they recognize the state's authority to restrict them from doing so.

As most readers are familiar, Hobbes endorses an extreme interpretation of this responsibility, arguing that almost any act of disobedience violates the individual's interest in maintaining their safety and security. Excluding those instances in which obeying the sovereign's command either explicitly involves self-harm or puts the individual in immediate danger (e.g., killing or maiming themselves, confessing to a crime, engaging in military combat), any form of insubordination

92 Post-Democratic Citizenship

would seem to weaken the power of the sovereign, thereby troubling the sovereign's ability to provide for the individual's own peace and defense.[36] As such, the individual has an overriding reason to obey any and all commands, even those that run counter to their other interests.

Yet, this interpretation appears uniquely indebted to the Hobbesian subject's understanding of their relationship to sovereignty, making it questionable as to whether the servant and, by extension, the post-democratic citizen should also understand themselves as having a similar degree of responsibility. Recall that, in covenanting with their fellow subjects to found the commonwealth, the subject sees the willingness, on the part of their neighbors and themself, to recognize the sovereign's authority as foundational for the exercise of sovereign power in general. Thus, the subject's disobedience not only challenges sovereign authority directly, but also the greater covenant deemed essential for sovereign authority in the first place. In this sense, it is not so much that the subject's disobedience could actually bring down the commonwealth, but that, in disobeying, the subject throws the basis of sovereign power into question in a way that may ultimately have noxious effects.

The servant's covenant, however, is hardly considered as essential for the commonwealth as a whole. Because the natural commonwealth is founded, not on a collective agreement, but on a multiplicity of bilateral covenants between the sovereign and individual servants, the dissolution of one or even a few of those covenants would not have nearly the same detrimental effects on sovereign power. In other words, whereas a neighbor's disobedience might have signaled to the Hobbesian subject that the covenant undergirding sovereign power was faltering, it suggests to the servant only that the neighbor has broken their particular covenant and, as such, would seem to have no effect on the sovereign's status from the servant's perspective. Moreover, the servant's understanding of sovereignty promotes the awareness that, while the covenant formalizes the sovereign's claim to authority, the real foundation of this claim is the sovereign's capacity for violence. Thus, disobedience, even when unpunished, does not pose nearly the same threat to sovereign power as a whole; only active instances of rebellion, in which private individuals attack the state directly, would challenge the servant's ability to rely on the sovereign for protection.

In drawing upon the model of the Hobbesian servant, the post-democratic citizen inherits a more complicated interpretation of political responsibility than the Hobbesian subject. Rather than understanding themselves as having a near-absolute duty to obey, post-democratic citizens are responsible to sovereign power only to the extent that disobedience would either invite some sort of violent or coercive reprisal or weaken the state to the point of ineffectiveness or collapse. Ultimately, the judgment as to the consequences of one's disobedience will be contextually dependent and probabilistic. Some crimes will go unnoticed; others will encourage the state to devote a substantial amount of time and resources to pursue and discipline the offender. Additionally, some individuals, by virtue of their class, race, gender, and so on, will be in a better position to avoid punishment.[37] In contrast with a democratic political logic, which, broadly speaking, only supports disobedience when it is construed as a form of political participation, non-violent, and used as a last resort, the post-democratic citizen has no such *prima facie* responsibility to first attempt to influence sovereign decision-making or refrain from violence; post-democratic domination puts the individual in a position where all they can do is distinguish between the laws they can follow and those they cannot and, taking into account the risks involved, act accordingly.

Finally, while democratic political participation implies a degree of culpability for the negative effects that may result from any given state policy or action that the democratic citizen must shoulder, as Hans-Jorg Sigwart puts it, "one's part of the moral guilt that politics necessarily involves," the post-democratic citizen should consider themself relieved of any such guilt.[38] Lacking any influence over sovereign power, they are neither in a position to contribute to political decision-making nor prevent the enactment of decisions already made; both their endorsements and condemnations are purely symbolic. As such, it is difficult to see how the post-democratic subject could be held responsible for the unfortunate, tragic, or atrocious consequences, unintended or otherwise, often linked with political outcomes. This list includes "collateral damage" from military strikes, direct attacks on civilians, the barbarous treatment of the undocumented, discriminatory practices, mass incarceration, economic policies that exacerbate inequality, and environmental destruction. Like a passenger on a runaway train, the post-democratic citizen has no ability to stop it from striking others, only the occasional, limited opportunity to warn those who may be in danger.

Hobbes, too, gives us good reason for disassociating the post-democratic citizen from the moral implications of both sovereign decision-making and the act of obeying those decisions. To find fault with the non-sovereign individuals in such instances would be to invite continuous political instability, brought on by regularly goading non-sovereign individuals to challenge or resist the state based on their "private judgments" "of good and evil actions."[39] Subsequently, Hobbes not only exempts non-sovereign individuals from any blame related to either the content of sovereign decisions or their repercussions, but absolves them from any guilt they may feel for actions they, personally, carry out in the sovereign's name. As Hobbes writes,

> that whatsoever a subject … is compelled to [do] in obedience to his sovereign, and doth in it not in order to his own mind, but in order to the laws of his country, that action is not his, but his sovereign's.[40]

Yet, as Edwin Curley points out in his edition of *Leviathan*, what makes Hobbes's position here so striking is that it seems in conflict with Hobbes's more general position that the non-sovereign individual has always-already authorized all

94 Post-Democratic Citizenship

sovereign actions, including those he may privately find objectionable; in short, one cannot help but bear responsibility, not only when obeying sovereign commands, but for all of the sovereign's decisions.[41] This would then seem to imply a deep reservoir of guilt traceable to that initial moment of consent. Still, the respective conditions distinguishing the Hobbesian subject's covenant from that of the servant are relevant here; in the subject's case, they could have avoided culpability by never covenanting with their neighbors in the first place; the servant only by embracing imprisonment or death. Though Hobbes appears somewhat inconsistent, *if* either's action warrants blame, the deliberate nature of the subject's covenant would seem more damning than the servant's decision to save their own skin.

To the extent that post-democratic citizens similarly lack any hand in the formation of sovereign power, but rather find themselves always-already dominated, leaving them with the option to either consent or suffer the consequences, it is difficult to saddle them with the sort of far-reaching liability more readily ascribed to the democratic citizen for actively choosing the former. This is not, however, to suggest that they have no choice but to look favorably on all state policies and actions; only that they need not consider them their own. For some, this sort of attitude may not sit well. The argument that post-democratic citizens should not feel guilty for decisions ostensibly made in their name challenges, not only the prevailing democratic tendency to stress the responsibility one has to govern (and, thus, govern well), but, moreover, the broader moral responsibilities one often feels toward others. Some may even go so far as to feel compelled to find fault with the servant's decision to consent in the first place, maintaining that the right choice would be refusal, despite the consequences of doing so. Thus, especially among the many still harboring remnants of a democratic political logic, there will be those who feel uncomfortable—to say the least—with simply jettisoning the guilt they may feel over sovereign decisions that harm others or, further, the feeling that one has a duty to do something about it.

Yet, whether attempting to alleviate the guilt that stems from the poor decisions made in one's name or the broader feelings of frustration, anxiety, and alienation characteristic of post-democratic life, abstractly theorizing one's relationship to political authority and activity can only do so much. In addition to being thought, post-democracy must be lived. In other words, achieving any sort of lasting therapeutic benefit depends upon realizing one's political subjectivity *practically*, going beyond treating one's political self-conception as a mere thought experiment and using it to make sense of one's lived experience. This requires critically interrogating and, if need be, addressing the narratives and concepts that frame one's inevitable involvement in the superficially democratic political practices that pervade post-democratic life. In short, to continue to think of oneself post-democratically when most susceptible to understanding oneself otherwise: when expressing one's preferences, voicing dissent, or discussing politics. In Chapter Six, I will bring a post-democratic outlook to bear on these activities, which, despite being unable to influence sovereign decision-making, provide opportunities for both attuning oneself to the greater consequences of post-democratic sovereignty and discovering the unique (often intangible), applied insights that enable one's life to take on an edifying and conciliatory intelligibility under political domination.

Notes

1 Pettit 2010, p. 52
2 Pettit 2010, p. 52
3 Pettit 2010, p. 56
4 Pettit 2010, p. 56
5 Pettit 2010, p. 56
6 Pettit 2010, pp. 56–57
7 For more on the idea of exit, see Hirschman 1970.
8 While, in the absence of democratic political procedures, it is clear why the relationship is not causal, the conditions under which public opinion is measured, both in the way polls can manipulate issue salience and one's recorded opinion on an issue, make any claims concerning correlation highly suspect.
9 Hobbes [1668] 1994, sec. XVI.4
10 Hobbes [1668] 1994, sec. II.XVII
11 Technically, one could make the case that he actually offers three models of political subjectivity, but it is questionable as to whether the "child" is inherently political or, rather, a private form of dominion.
12 Hobbes [1668] 1994, sec. XVII.13, XX.10
13 David Hume [1738] 1994, pp. 167–168
14 To this end, Pettit sharply criticizes Hobbes's understanding of liberty (as non-interference) and instead proposes a model of freedom as non-domination. While more reliant on the courts than the ballot box, even Pettit's republicanism would seem to require a degree of political equality absent under post-democracy. See Pettit 2010, p. 41.
15 Gauthier 1969, pp. 116–117. Gauthier later goes on to argue that, for this very reason, Hobbes made a mistake in politically equating the two. Yet, it could just as easily be that the theory of authorization Gauthier wants to ascribe to Hobbes is just a distraction from Hobbes's deeper point concerning the domination inherent in political life.
16 Hobbes [1668] 1994, sec. XX.3
17 Hobbes [1668] 1994, sec. XIII.9
18 Hobbes [1668] 1994, sec. XVII.13
19 Hobbes [1668] 1994, sec. XX.10
20 Hobbes [1668] 1994, sec. XX.12
21 One could argue, as Jean Hampton does, that regardless of *how* one joins the commonwealth, it ultimately represents an improvement over continuing to live under a state of war. Yet, it is hardly a given that the servant's violent subjugation will appear as such to her, who may have failed to find fault in her anarchic context or, even if she did not, preferred it to life under a sovereign power. See Hampton 1988, p. 172.
22 See Anderson 1991.
23 Hobbes [1668] 1994, sec. XVII.13
24 Hobbes [1668] 1994, sec. XVII.15
25 Hobbes [1668] 1994, sec. XX.2
26 Strauss 1952, p. 67. Notably, in *The Elements of the Law*, Hobbes explicitly associates the artificial commonwealth with a democratic foundation; see Hobbes [1640] 1969, part II, ch. 2, sec. 1.

96 Post-Democratic Citizenship

27 Strauss 1952, p. 66
28 Strauss 1952, p. 64
29 Hobbes [1640] 1969, part II, ch. 4, sec. 9. In *De Cive*, he also argues that subjects "perform more honourable services within the commonwealth ... and enjoy more luxuries," but his distinction here seems to reflect differences in economic rather than political status. See Hobbes [1642] 1998, ch. 9, sec. 9.
30 Hobbes [1668] 1994, sec. XVIII.6–8. One may object here that the sovereign's decision to spare the servant's life actually implies a direct contract between the two of them, one which requires the sovereign to protect the servant as long as the servant obeys. While I personally read Hobbes differently, if the sovereign did take on certain obligations when covenanting with the servant, it is questionable how the servant would ever enforce them. The sovereign's failure to satisfy those obligations might then give the servant the right to revolt, but what good is a right without the capacity to effectively exercise it?
31 This is not at all to suggest that sovereign power cannot have a positive impact on the life of the post-democratic citizen, only that this impact is so divorced from democratic practice as to make it unpredictable and wholly contingent; though it may be a cause for celebration, the realization of one's political preferences should not contribute to any sort of hope in post-democratic sovereignty itself.
32 Hobbes [1668] 1994, sec. XVIII.2, XX.11
33 For those able to wield political influence, however, membership would still be a question of participation, not in a democratic process, but in the domination of others.
34 Hobbes [1668] 1994, sec. XXIV.7; in his earlier work, *The Elements of the Law*, he makes the point explicit for servants as well. See Hobbes [1640] 1969, part II, ch. 3, sec. 4.
35 See Rawls 1971, pp. 513–520
36 Hobbes [1668] 1994, sec. XXI.11–16
37 This is hardly to suggest that these sorts of privileges should be celebrated, but only to recognize the way in which they can and should factor into the post-democratic citizen's assessment of their ability to disregard sovereign command.
38 Sigwart 2013, p. 432
39 Hobbes [1668] 1994, sec. XXIX, sec. 6. See also XXIX.7.
40 Hobbes [1668] 1994, sec. XLII.11
41 Hobbes [1668] 1994, p. 339, fn12

References

Anderson, Benedict. *The Imagined Community*. London: Verso Press, 1991.
Gauthier, David. *The Logic of Leviathan*. New York: Oxford UP, 1969.
Hampton, Jean. *Hobbes and the Social Contract Tradition*. New York: Cambridge UP, 1988.
Hirschman, Albert. *Exit, Voice, and Loyalty: Responses to Decline in Firms, Organizations, and States*. Cambridge, MA: Harvard UP, 1970.
Hobbes, Thomas. *The Elements of Law; Natural and politic*. London: Frank Cass, [1640] 1969.
Hobbes, Thomas. *On the Citizen*. New York: Cambridge UP, [1642] 1998.
Hobbes, Thomas. *Leviathan*. Indianapolis, IN: Hackett Publishing, [1668] 1994.
Hume, David. "Of the Original Contract" in *Political Writings*. Stuart Warner and Donald Livingston, eds. Indianapolis, IN: Hackett Publishing, [1738] 1994.
Pettit, Philip. *Republicanism*. New York: Oxford UP, 2010.
Rawls, John. *A Theory of Justice*. Cambridge, MA: Harvard UP, 1971.
Sigwart, Hans-Jorg. "The Logic of Legitimacy: Ethics in Political Realism," *The Review of Politics* 75. 3 (Summer 2013): 407–432.
Strauss, Leo. *The Political Philosophy of Hobbes: Its Basis and Its Genesis*. Chicago: University of Chicago Press, 1952.

6

POST-DEMOCRATIC PARTICIPATION

In the last two chapters, we explored the broader implications of a post-democratic diagnosis for the reading and writing of political philosophy; namely, a redirection away from the question of how ordinary citizens ought to best exercise political influence (practico-political approach) and toward the question of how they can best endure the political power exercised by others (therapeutic approach). In this chapter, we examine the further implications of a post-democratic diagnosis for the myriad forms of superficially democratic, (pseudo-)political forms of participation that make up post-democratic life: the expression of political preference (including voting), protest, and political discussion. The unforgiving irony of post-democratic life is that these sort of mass activities routinely fail to facilitate the sort of free, deliberate exercise of political power they otherwise purport to enable, but they nonetheless persist unchanged. Despite their inability to affect political outcomes in a manner consistent with democratic values, this chapter argues that these activities can serve a uniquely therapeutic purpose, enabling citizens to work through their own experience of political powerlessness within a familiar set of social practices and rituals. Rather than simply withdraw from (pseudo-)political activities or separate an awareness of one's political powerlessness from their participation in them (i.e., compartmentalization), ordinary citizens should repurpose these activities to address the distinct consequences—frustration, anxiety, and alienation—of a post-democratic present.

After discussing two alternative approaches to post-democratic politics (withdrawal and compartmentalization), I will offer a theory of therapeutic (pseudo-) political participation drawn primarily from recent accounts of Paul Kingsnorth's Dark Mountain Project, an apocalyptic environmental group dedicated to mourning the irreversible consequences of rampant development and climate change. By making use of ostensibly political practices like expression, protest, and discussion to deal with the grief surrounding their inability to save/protect the planet, the Dark Mountain Project illustrates how self-aware post-democratic citizens can similarly adapt such practices to confront their own failure as democratic citizens and negotiate a new kind of political self-understanding. I will then turn to a discussion of the various ways these practices may be adapted so that ordinary citizens can use them to start to rethink their role in an enduring, speciously democratic political culture; to figure out, in practice, what it is to *act* like a post-democratic citizen. I will conclude by turning to the broader political implications of adopting a post-democratic self-conception; specifically, by asking whether a post-democratic outlook necessarily implies a kind of conservatism or even an apology for authoritarianism. Ultimately, I suggest that a post-democratic outlook—far from a defense of post-democratic conditions—instead constitutes a form of political realism, one oriented toward overcoming the obstructive prejudices of a myopic commitment to democracy and, subsequently, more radical than one might initially suspect.

Three Approaches to (Pseudo-)Political Activity

Post-democratic sovereignty distinguishes itself from other forms of domination through its reliance on a democratic political imaginary, one which encourages ordinary citizens to think of themselves as political actors despite their demonstrable lack of political influence. Districts are increasingly gerrymandered, corporate money flows, and economic elites continue to win out, but elections are still touted as an opportunity for popular sovereignty and society at large speaks as if political equality has either been achieved or will be soon. By consistently involving ordinary citizens in a myriad of negligible ways, all parties—elites, bureaucrats, and the governed—can behave as if the demos really speaks, maintaining the fantasy, as Zizek would say, of a democratic polity.[1]

Moreover, as discussed in Chapter Two, the weight of this democratic political imaginary is not felt intermittently, as if present only during election cycles or otherwise historic moments, but all the time. In the way they think, speak, and act with one another, self-understood democratic citizens treat each other as if they do or, at the very least, should have a meaningful say in sovereign decision-making by affording one another the basic dignity of consideration, while also expecting one another to fulfill certain civic responsibilities foundational for and flowing from the exercise of political power.[2] Even when not explicitly discussing political issues, these underlying assumptions about the state's democratic credentials have profound implications for how citizens think about state legitimacy, their membership in a national community, their responsibility to that community/the state, and their culpability for its actions. When these assumptions are no longer tenable, it raises the question: how should self-aware post-democratic citizens think about their involvement in (or abstention from) the myriad of

Post-Democratic Participation **99**

practices and habits that make up a predominantly democratic culture? How should they respond to consistently being treated and addressed *as if* they really are democratic citizens?

One option would be to entirely withdraw from these sorts of (pseudo-)political activities on principle. After all, why continue to pretend? Why bother? Why participate (e.g., vote, protest) knowing it has no effect? Why even discuss or pay attention to politics knowing that one's preferences will ultimately be disregarded, assuming they are even acknowledged in the first place? Understandably, the idea of democratic failure should probably generate a fair amount of resentment as well, making the prospect of withdrawal seem even more desirable as it enables citizens to avoid having to think about it. Additionally, citizens could find some solace in no longer contributing to the democratic imaginary that sustains post-democracy. There is also the further hope that, if this refusal is recognized as it is intended, others may follow the example and withdraw as well, possibly even hastening the system's transformation or collapse through a broad campaign of non-participation, perhaps even non-cooperation (though, at present, this seems highly unlikely).

Alternatively, citizens could attempt to compartmentalize their awareness of political powerlessness, separating it from their regular involvement in (pseudo-) political activity in such a way that allows them to continue said involvement. Distinct from the sort of ironic participation described briefly in Chapter Four, one in which the individual perversely enjoys the faking and/or parodying democratic citizenship, this would be a kind of incoherent involvement, one in which the individual is aware of post-democratic conditions, but continues to participate out of habit, social pressure, or some ambiguous sense of obligation. As Zizek highlights, this is precisely what maintains the fantasy of democratic citizenship, but is it not also a reasonable response to having few other options? In fact, the more far-fetched fantasy may be believing that one might successfully encourage either greater participation or, as in the case of withdrawal, greater non-participation to such an extent that conditions change. Instead, why not simply 'lean into' post-democracy, recognizing the historico-political conditions of one's society as largely insurmountable and deciding to enjoy the available democratic culture, even if superficial, for what it is? Moreover, there is always the possibility that, if one just keeps showing up, things may change for the better, so why not?[3] In the meantime, this position allows one to feel as if *something* is being done, even if that something ends up being politically irrelevant.

Yet, the problem with both withdrawal and compartmentalization is that rather than seeking to engage with a post-democratic present, they aim to escape it or avoid thinking about it all together. Compartmentalization attempts to ignore this reality completely, bracketing the brute fact of post-democracy, but this strategy becomes less tenable when in the governing minority and more regularly subject to political outcomes at odds with one's preference. In other words, this sort of compartmentalization is a kind of privilege uniquely available to those who, by and large, tend to win out anyway, never having to confront the more explicit consequences of political powerlessness. The other option, withdrawal, at least formally acknowledges a condition of political powerlessness, but still tries to evade it through a symbolic separation, one which, by giving up any claim to political power, hopes to relieve the feeling of being dominated. Withdrawal tries to bury frustration by championing alienation and alleviate anxiety by encouraging the disposition of the dispassionate observer, careful not to get caught up in the terrifying banalities of contemporary political life. That is unless, of course, these feelings are considered one's cross to bear, the wages of a collective inability to realize democratic values.[4] This distance could provide some relief, but only at the price of a deeper isolation from one's world. As such, neither position is able to directly confront the reality of a post-democratic present, preventing self-aware post-democratic citizens from making sense of either the lived experience of domination or the resulting feelings of frustration, anxiety, and alienation.

There is a third option. Rather than either unproductively fixating on the absence of democratic practice or actively ignoring it, one can try to address those feelings of frustration, anxiety, and alienation by, first, validating them, and second, shaping one's engagement with (pseudo-) political activity in such a way that these concerns are at the forefront. Primarily, this involves developing a new ethical disposition (i.e., a new *ethos*) or subjectivity, as Foucault would say, in relation to the broader political concerns that animate one's distress; finding a new way of relating and acting in a world that intends, not to realize a better world, but to confront the sin of being a failed democratic citizen.

Perhaps the best introduction to this approach is by way of example. From 2010 to 2013, the Dark Mountain Project, a network of environmental activists, writers, academics, and artists, held an annual event in the United Kingdom called "Uncivilization." Rather than meeting to discuss what they could do to protect the environment, they instead gathered for a very different purpose. Through workshops, panels, performance art, and ritualized practice, they mourned the destruction of the Earth. As one of the group's founders, Paul Kingsnorth, explains, activism had failed to slow, much less stop, the ongoing destruction of the planet, raising the question of whether such efforts were really worthwhile.

> Everything had gotten worse … You look at every trend that environmentalists like me have been trying to stop for 50 years, and every single thing had gotten worse. And I thought: I can't do this anymore. I can't sit here saying: "Yes, comrades, we must act! We only need one more push, and we'll save the world!" I don't believe it. I don't believe it! So what do I do?[5]

"Uncivilization" can be understood as one way of responding to this feeling of powerlessness, one which directly confronts its consequences by, as Naomi Klein observes, giving "people a forum in which to be honest about their sense of dread

Post-Democratic Participation **101**

and loss."[6] The festival and, more generally, Dark Mountain allow people the chance to collectively address the question of

> What do you do … when you accept that all of these changes are coming, things that you value are going to be lost, things that make you unhappy are going to happen, things that you wanted to achieve you can't achieve, but you still have to live with it, and there's still beauty, and there's still meaning, and there are still things you can do to make the world less bad?[7]

As Kingsnorth elaborates further, these are not

> a series of questions that have any answers other than people's personal answers to them. Selfishly it's just a process I'm going through … It's extremely narcissistic of me. Rather than just having a personal crisis, I've said: "Hey! Come share my crisis with me!"[8]

Akin to the crisis experienced by Rome's former governing class in the wake of the Republic's fall, Kingsnorth's 'personal crisis' falls under the broader category of Foucault's "crisis of subjectivation" discussed in Chapter Four.[9] Previously, Kingsnorth understood himself as an environmental activist; as such, 'environmentalism' provided an ethical framework through which he could structure his sense of value.[10] In spreading awareness about climate change or protesting overdevelopment, he could feel as if his life had greater meaning, giving him a sense of existential fulfillment. However, this self-conception depended on the modest assumption that his actions would have some level of impact; that, despite setbacks and obstacles, things could get better. When that assumption proved unfounded, Kingsnorth's ethical framework became disrupted, leaving him feeling disoriented and distraught. The Dark Mountain Project, thus, can be understood as his attempt to work through those feelings by trying to discover a way to move forward, not by seeking out new forms of environmental activism, but by reconceptualizing the ethical framework that previously informed his attachment to activism in the first place. In short, a way of reconciling one's sense of self with an unfamiliar and/or perverted landscape. No longer able to see himself as a participant in political activity, Kingsnorth instead began to think of himself in a new light, as having a duty to bear witness to the Earth's destruction and, subsequently, to grieve. In doing so, he embraced a new model of ethical subjectivity, one he was not only able to realize, but that further gave his existence a new sense of purpose, however grim that purpose may be.

It is precisely this kind of ethical re-constitution that lies at the core of a therapeutic approach to (pseudo-)political involvement: repurposing (pseudo-)political activity as a way of transforming one's understanding of oneself rather than the world at large. To use such activities as a way of making sense of the world and one's relationship to it, a way of developing a more coherent understanding of one's own political existence, an understanding able to generate a sense of familiarity and, hence, provide some degree of relief under otherwise unsettling conditions. Instead of trying to realize a particular political outcome (i.e., greater environmental protections), Kingsnorth participated in a host of ostensibly political practices—writing manifestos, organizing gatherings, and spreading awareness—in order to develop a new self-understanding able to accommodate both his existential attachment to environmentalism and his political irrelevance. In other words, he took activities traditionally associated with sovereign decision-making and used them as a means of alleviating his own 'personal crisis;' what was once political became therapeutic. His deep connections with such practices allowed him to recognize the ways in which life can 'go on' despite the trauma of powerlessness. The realization of his own political insignificance didn't have to radically transform his form of life (i.e., the activities in which he engaged), but only the meaning he gave to it; he could still write, speak, and associate with others—in short, *act* politically—even though he remained unable to influence environmental policy. This renewed sense of purpose helped him overcome his general sense of disorientation by freeing him to once again find himself in the activities that mattered most to him, only now with a newfound interpretation of their value.

Furthermore, a new self-understanding can help mitigate feelings of failure and despair resulting from a lack of political influence by validating them. Much in the same way recognizing oneself as perpetually late or a klutz can lessen feelings of anxiety or frustration that may result from being tardy or clumsy, embracing one's own powerlessness can diminish the severity of *feeling* powerless, though, of course, not the severity of *being* powerless, which is precisely what the citizen must learn to cope with. It allows them to 'own' the experience, as it were, to call it what it is, and to begin to develop strategies that could allow the citizen to endure. Though perhaps unable to overcome these feelings—to feel, as it were, empowered and optimistic—individuals can find a way to live *with them* that relies on neither cognitive dissonance nor withdrawal, but rather through a sober confrontation with the conditions faced and a willingness to adapt accordingly. Moreover, to the extent that others are found that share this willingness (e.g., the Dark Mountain Project), there is the possibility of finding community in it as well, which may alleviate some of the alienation inherent in a lonely recognition of powerlessness.

What would it be, then, to refashion one's political involvement in light of a post-democratic diagnosis? While Kingsnorth was not confronting the experience of post-democracy *per se*, he was certainly responding to a version of it (i.e., lack of influence over environmental policy) and, more generally speaking, the feelings of frustration, anxiety, and alienation intrinsic to it. As such, his example illustrates the unique value of the therapeutic approach to political involvement for post-democratic life. Though most individuals are not as politically involved as Kingsnorth, to live in a modern, Western "democracy" is to be accustomed to the host of activities and expectations that make up the fabric of democratic life.

In providing a way for individuals to process those sorts of feelings through the (pseudo-)political practices with which they are already familiar, a therapeutic approach allows them to engage with the more quotidian consequences of post-democratic sovereignty. It provides an opportunity for citizens to reconcile their lived experience in a ubiquitous democratic political imaginary with an awareness of their own domination; to figure out how to be a self-aware post-democrat in a context in which everyone is consistently treated as if they were a democratic citizen.

Post-Democracy in Practice

What would this look like? Let's examine three possible post-democratic re-appropriations of (pseudo-)political activity: the expression of political preference, dissent, and political discussion.

First, the expression of political preference is typically understood to be essential for—if not synonymous with—democratic political activity; popular sovereignty follows from the *demos*'s ability to direct sovereign decision-making by voicing considered opinions. Forms of expression include wearing political attire, sporting bumper stickers, posting yard signs, publishing one's opinions (including on Facebook, Twitter, etc.), drafting/signing petitions, and, of course, voting. Yet, under post-democratic conditions, the expressed preferences of ordinary citizens end up falling upon deaf ears or, in the case of voting, remain constrained by elite preferences, effectively inhibiting the citizen's ability to independently influence sovereign decision-making. From a post-democratic perspective, however, these sorts of activities can take on a new significance, one no longer tied to the exercise of political influence, but to a new kind of ethical self-realization. By providing ordinary citizens an opportunity to actualize their political identities, identify with genuine political actors, and find solidarity with friends, neighbors, and countless anonymous others (both online and in person), the expression of political preference can provide real therapeutic benefits under post-democratic conditions by alleviating feelings of alienation and anxiety.

Through participation in culturally significant practices like voting or wearing a T-shirt with a political slogan or symbol, individuals can realize themselves as a particular kind of political subject (e.g., as opposed or for something) despite not having the power to realize their preferences. For example, voting for environmental protections gives an individual the chance to actualize themself as an environmentalist; similarly, wearing an anti-racist T-shirt lets one assume the identity of an anti-racist. It is a way of embodying a value or principle in spite of one's political powerlessness.[11] All in all, the relationship between identity and activity in these instances is largely arbitrary; one need not vote to consider oneself an environmentalist, nor wear the right clothing in order to be against racism. Still, as in any sort of ritualized practice, the activity takes on the significance with which we impute it. One may consider oneself a Christian without having been

104 Post-Democratic Participation

baptized, but the practice certainly has the effect of making one feel 'official,' as well as communicating that identity to others.

By allowing the individual to realize a particular kind of identity, the expression of political preference further lets the individual identify with a particular political movement, faction, or leader. Again, this is not to say that ordinary citizens are able to influence sovereign decision-making in any significant sense, that they assume the role of a political actor. Rather, it is simply that they are able to declare their sympathies, establishing a remote, symbolic connection with those actually engaging in political activity. Here, the comparison to being a sports fan is helpful. When supporters wear a jersey or root for their team, they do not actively influence the outcome of the game. They remain merely spectators. Yet, the act of wearing the jersey or cheering allows them to identify with the team, to express an existential connection with the team's efforts, and to further emotionally invest themselves in the team's victory or defeat. While hardly replicating the experience of being on the pitch (or even the sidelines), post-democratic political expression amounts to a form of vicarious participation, one that allows ordinary citizens to establish an imagined bond with genuine political actors.

Finally, the expression of preference gives ordinary citizens the opportunity to feel in solidarity with other non-elites who share their views; to bond, as it were, with other fans. From a democratic perspective, this sense of solidarity is instrumentally valuable to the degree that it correlates with increased levels of political participation. From a post-democratic perspective, however, the value lies in helping to alleviate feelings of alienation that stem from a general lack of political community. To wear a political T-shirt, write about politics online, or even vote should be considered a way, not of actually influencing politics, but of signaling to others that they are not alone.[12] It is the practical equivalent of asking "Do you see what I see?", which, in turn, can help relieve the sense that one's judgment or worldview is hopelessly distorted or detached. In the absence of Arendtian public spaces and Habermasian deliberative practices, it offers a way of connecting with others that, despite not being political, helps us to feel less isolated and, subsequently, less uneasy.

Dissent, particularly when voiced collectively, constitutes a special case of political expression. Whereas self-aware post-democratic citizens abstractly know that they are unable to influence politics, dissent highlights the specific repercussions (e.g., the new war, the new law, the failed response, etc.) of their powerlessness. By confronting them with the consequences of their powerlessness, dissent gives these citizens an opportunity to truly recognize themselves as a failed democratic citizen, demonstrating how their dissatisfaction, incredulity, or outrage are exhausted in their expression. In doing so, it concretizes the effects of political insignificance. As such, dissent becomes an opportunity, not to reverse a course of action or to speak truth to power, but to mourn particular failings and the conditions of post-democracy as a whole.[13] On the one hand, in a way made explicit by the Dark Mountain Project, dissent allows the individual to mourn a particular decision or response. In this sense, it provides an emotional outlet to vent one's sense of loss, as well as the frustrations and anxiety that surround it. On the other hand, dissent gives individuals the chance to mourn their general sense of powerlessness, the experience of post-democratic political subjectivity as a whole; to mourn either a democracy lost or one never adequately realized. Through this process, individuals can begin to explore the affective consequences of their domination, the troubling feelings that result from an inability to live up to democratic ideals that not only pervade one's society, but continue to have personal or even existential significance.

Engaging in political discussion further enables a confrontation with democratic failure, but with the additional advantage of allowing individuals to explicitly reckon with the everyday consequences of their political insignificance. This breaks dramatically with a democratic understanding of political discussion, which characterizes it either as a preliminary step to forming a considered preference (that one will then attempt to realize) or as a form of political activity in itself. Rather than focusing on what 'We' ought to do when making sovereign decisions, a post-democratic approach to political discussion treats it as an opportunity to consider what it means to lack democratic political practice. In other words, for ordinary citizens to intersubjectively explore the experience of political powerlessness, as well as what it means to no longer be part of a 'We.'

On a practical level, such discussions allow individuals to share strategies for responding to the political decisions made by others, to develop ways of enduring or resisting sovereign power. For instance, in the event a law is passed that allows for individuals to carry concealed firearms, those concerned can work to identify public places less likely to attract armed individuals; if the state decides to ramp up the enforcement of immigration policies, individuals can discuss ways to help shield their neighbors from harassment and exile, like, for instance, not calling the police to the scene of an accident if an undocumented individual is involved.[14] Still, this is not to suggest that all sovereign decisions will admit some possibility for resistance; some, especially budgetary or foreign policy decisions, will leave individuals no choice but to abide. After all, *contra* John Lennon and Yoko Ono's famous pronouncement, wanting peace is not enough to stop the war. Even still, individuals can talk about ways of making such decisions easier to bear, either through painting them in a different light or finding ways to get around them.

Moreover, through regularly having these sorts of discussions, ordinary citizens can cultivate a more practical orientation toward the lived experience of post-democratic citizenship; they can develop a deeper appreciation of the more quotidian consequences of political powerlessness. Rather than simply thinking through questions of legitimacy, membership, responsibility, and culpability alone, discussing political concerns from a post-democratic perspective allows them to take on a deeper fullness, one only possible when citizens *collectively* think through the real implications of taking such positions and hold one another

106 Post-Democratic Participation

accountable for them. In short, post-democratic discussion can and should both check and guide our thinking on post-democracy. These discussions enable citizens to hash out what such conditions mean for their functional relationship with particular institutions like the police, the courts, and other state institutions in a way that is not merely hypothetical, but applied. For instance, when is it justified to reach out to law enforcement, knowing that the laws they enforce are not the will of the People, but the will of the few? Should citizens respect the results of elections in gerrymandered districts or referendums largely determined by public relations campaigns, or instead find ways to subvert or ignore these specious examples of popular sovereignty? And to what extent should citizens honor and incorporate the various national symbols and texts (e.g., flags, anthems, constitutions) with which they are familiar after these items have lost their former democratic character?

Finally, the practice of discussion is particularly helpful for addressing questions of culpability. While citizens may be able to dispassionately maintain a lack of culpability for state actions in general, they may have a more complicated response when discussing the specific consequences of those actions with others, one that draws their attention to the more intractable remnants of their former democratic outlook. In this sense, talking about specific instances of powerlessness and their real-world repercussions can enable individuals to confront and explore the shame of being a nominal democratic citizen, not in order to rationalize their condition, but to cathartically process the ongoing implications of it. How, for example, should self-professed democratic citizens respond to their essentially passive role in relation to a non-democratic state? How should they reconcile paying their taxes, having respect for the law, teaching their children to honor state authorities, and otherwise failing to actively reform or oppose the state with their principled commitment to popular sovereignty and political equality? How should the few justify privilege in a non-democratic society? Should they even try? And to what extent should citizens be condemned for living an incoherent or fractured political existence?

There are no easy answers to these questions; there may not even be satisfying ones. The prospect of democratic failure is hardly one that can (or perhaps should) be resolved quickly, but by developing a more robust practical orientation toward the experience of political domination, specifically by continuing to engage in (pseudo-)political life from a therapeutic perspective, ordinary citizens can better familiarize themselves with—and habituate themselves to—the more subtle contours of post-democratic life. Hopefully, these efforts can assist in facilitating a more coherent political self-understanding, one not at odds with post-democracy, but appropriate to it, and tempering the frustration, anxiety, and alienation that stem from political insignificance by enabling individuals to become used to it. By normalizing this condition, transforming it from a profound and distressing failure to, quite literally, 'politics as usual,' discussion can allow citizens to process the conditions in which they find themselves, helping them feel less disoriented and, subsequently, more 'at home' in an effort to reign in the levels of uncertainty and unease that contribute to said feelings and enable citizens to better cope with the peculiar experience of political powerlessness that distinguishes post-democratic life.

Whether such activities will ultimately be therapeutic remains an empirical question, one which will inevitably vary from person to person. For some, withdrawal or compartmentalization may be a better way forward, if only to avoid the rather ugly reality of post-democratic sovereignty. They may think: if there is truly nothing to be done, perhaps it is best to do nothing or, at least, nothing different. There may not be a definitive means of convincing them otherwise. But for those unsatisfied with this approach, those unwilling to either bracket or simply forget the matter, and feel the need to more deeply reflect on their political standing and the implications of it, the time spent engaging in these sorts of (pseudo-)political activities would seem to provide the ideal opportunity for such reflection. In conjunction with a therapeutic approach to political philosophy as a whole, it may even yield a persuasively better way of comporting oneself within a post-democratic present, which may be the only present any of us ever get.

The Politics of Post-Democracy

This approach raises one obvious question: what are the political implications of treating (pseudo-)political activity as a primarily therapeutic practice, prioritizing self-understanding and individual well-being over the exercise of political influence? What of the post-democratic outlook as a whole? Is it a left-wing position? A right-wing one? Or something different entirely?

In concluding, this chapter will discuss the ways in which a post-democratic outlook provides a way of thinking about politics that reveal the limitations inherent in simply focusing on political preferences, instead encouraging us to marry preference with context in order to paint a fuller picture of one's relationship with political authority and activity. In this sense, it is best understood as part of the broader, contemporary realist turn in political theory, most commonly associated with Bernard Williams and Raymond Geuss. In the end, through reimagining legitimacy, membership, responsibility, and culpability in light of pervasive political domination, a post-democratic outlook offers a more fertile and, hence, progressive approach than its democratic counterpart to *both* political and (pseudo-)political activity.

What, then, does a post-democratic diagnosis imply about an ordinary citizen's political beliefs? Whether employing the traditional left-right spectrum or one of the more popular two-dimensional models (e.g., the Political Compass, Nolan Chart, Pournelle Chart, etc.), placing a post-democratic outlook on a political spectrum presents a challenge. This is because the only substantive political preference deducible from a post-democratic outlook is a sympathy toward popular sovereignty and political equality. Otherwise, it has no bearing on one's greater

108 Post-Democratic Participation

political preferences. One could easily be a rightwing post-democrat or a leftwing post-democrat, libertarian or statist, liberal or traditionalist, and so on.[15] Friedrich Hayek's two-dimensional political spectrum gives us a bit more purchase, but still not enough.[16] In it, he distinguishes between one's preference as to the scope of sovereign decision-making, whether one is a liberal (limited scope) or a totalitarian (extended scope), and one's preferred decision-making practice, whether one is a democrat (inclusive) or an authoritarian (exclusive). According to this model, the self-aware post-democratic, while open to being liberal or totalitarian, would express a clear preference for democratic decision-making practices, despite being pessimistic as to the possibility of their realization.

Insofar as only political preferences are measured, not political *self*-conceptions, such spectrums (including Hayek's) remain of limited value.[17] Rather, we would need a political spectrum able to distinguish the two, between what ordinary citizens want and how they understand their involvement in pursuit of those preferences. This could constitute an additional axis, able to be added to any of the more traditional spectra, that specifies not what the individual wants out of politics, but the individual's faith in their ability to decide political outcomes, extending from the democratic believer to the post-democratic skeptic. On a more fundamental level, however, a post-democratic diagnosis calls into question the *political* value of such identifications, at least among ordinary citizens, which in turn raises the question: what does it matter as to the *political* implications of a therapeutic approach if the approaches taken by ordinary citizens have no bearings on politics to begin with?

One could argue that, despite professing an ostensible respect for democratic values, a post-democratic outlook ironically commits citizens to an authoritarian position through encouraging a fatalistic political quietism. The idea is that conceptualizing oneself as politically powerless makes one powerless, ensuring post-democratic sovereignty through pervasive apathy. This would, first, be to assume that ordinary citizens could exercise political influence any less than they already do under post-democratic conditions, but second, this accusation grossly mischaracterizes the post-democratic approach to (pseudo-)political activity. As discussed above, rather than prescribing withdrawal, it counsels a therapeutic engagement that, in many ways, results in the same exercise of political influence as more 'sincere' or politically motivated approaches to participation. In short, one's actions remain the same, only their interpretations change. Whether one votes explicitly to consecrate an aspect of one's identity or in the (vain) hope of influencing policy, there is no difference in political effect. Moreover, by highlighting the therapeutic value of such practices, it may actually encourage those who, perhaps due to their own political disaffection, have previously avoided them.

However, one could further argue that a post-democratic outlook limits an individual's *potential* commitment to political activity by encouraging them to think exclusively in terms of (pseudo-)political activity. For example, because self-aware post-democratic citizens privilege the therapeutic value of protest, those citizens may consciously abstain from involving themselves further (e.g., joining the association, planning other events). This would perhaps prevent these citizens from ever getting to a point where they are able to exercise a non-negligible degree of political influence.[18] On the one hand, this charge is warranted; treating (pseudo-)political activity as a therapeutic practice troubles the ability to see it as a kind of training for real political activity. On the other hand, by highlighting the superficiality of many activities otherwise assumed to be politically relevant, a post-democratic outlook forces us to reconsider what sorts of activities truly qualify as political. Subsequently, it also pushes would-be political actors to more seriously reflect on the value of certain activities, as well as whether they themselves are willing to make the sorts of commitments necessary to actually have a chance of influencing political outcomes. In doing so, it may encourage some ordinary citizens to dedicate themselves further than they would have otherwise had they held onto democratic assumptions about voting and other low-level forms of participation. By recognizing just how little democratic possibility these sorts of (pseudo-)political activities offer, citizens can take it upon themselves to find better avenues for influence.

Furthermore, by profoundly reconfiguring assumptions about legitimacy, membership, responsibility, and culpability, a post-democratic outlook also frees genuine political actors from the constraints of democratic political norms, allowing them to embrace more creative forms of political action.[19] No longer concerned about state legitimacy and, hence, the legitimacy of formal political practice, the post-democratic actor is free to manipulate such practices (e.g., discourse, elections, etc.), much in the same way elite political actors do repeatedly. The post-democratic citizen's instrumental conception of political membership and responsibility only further encourages this strategic openness to new and/or more Machiavellian ways of exercising political influence. Lastly, in distancing themselves from sovereign decisions and the guilt and/or shame that accompany them, post-democratic political actors relieve themselves of any general political responsibility toward fixing the polis and remain free to focus only on those issues which they feel best able to address. Thus, in the event they are able to exercise political influence, post-democratic citizens can do so radically unfettered.

Whether addressing political actors or those who will—at best—only engage in (pseudo-)political activity, a post-democratic outlook toward political authority and activity dispenses with the fantasy of a democratic political community in favor of a deeper understanding of one's own political environment. In this sense, it falls within the greater tradition of political realism, classically associated with Thucydides and Machiavelli, as well as more contemporary works by Bernard Williams, Raymond Geuss, and Jeffrey Green.[20] In fact, the post-democratic critique could easily be read as a version of Williams's broader charge against political moralism.[21] In it, Williams argues against any conceptual model of politics which makes "the moral prior to the political" and thereby obscures what is uniquely *political* about political activity; in particular, its often

110 Post-Democratic Participation

amoral, if not immoral, dimensions.[22] Similarly, a post-democratic outlook encourages one to dispense with the moral presumptions of popular sovereignty and political equality and instead recognize the profound disparities in political influence that have and will continue to affect the exercise of sovereign power. For some, this may constitute a call for a more serious dedication to politics, one which recognizes that voting, protesting, or generating discussion is not enough. For most, however, it will enable them to better conceptualize their relationship with political authority and activity, ideally letting them work through the frustration, anxiety, and alienation pervasive in contemporary post-democratic societies. In either case, to remain wedded to a democratic outlook toward politics, oddly enough, constitutes a sort of conservatism, a dated epistemic commitment that impedes a more relevant approach to politics. Instead, individuals must take the radical step of recognizing their own fractured relationship to post-democratic sovereignty, inciting their political imagination anew.

Notes

1 See Zizek 1989, pp. 11–53.
2 This 'basic dignity of consideration' is in effect often obstructed by systemic, but at times also explicit, forms of racism, sexism, homophobia, and other forms of discrimination and oppression, but the gesture itself—recognizing the value of majority opinion, counting the preference of those who one may disagree with, even hate—is indicative of deep democratic assumptions about the good society.
3 Note that, despite sharing the same goal, this strategy and the one described above would actively work against one another.
4 Cf. Adorno 2005, #5. "Sociability itself is a participant in injustice, insofar as it pretends we can still talk with each other in a frozen world, and the flippant, chummy word contributes to the perpetuation of silence, insofar as the concessions to those being addressed debase the latter once more as speakers ... For intellectuals, unswerving isolation is the only form in which they can vouchsafe a measure of solidarity. All of the playing along, all of the humanity of interaction and participation is the mere mask of the tacit acceptance of inhumanity. One should be united with the suffering of human beings: the smallest step to their joys is one towards the hardening of suffering."
5 Smith 2014
6 Smith 2014
7 Smith 2014
8 Smith 2014
9 Foucault 1986, p. 95
10 Unless Kingsnorth was *singularly* committed to environmental change, we would expect his sense of value to depend on other considerations (e.g., familial, professional, etc.) as well.
11 Cf. Arendt [1958] 1998, sec. V, particularly the idea of action as principled self-disclosure. Arendt presupposes a public space in which such self-disclosure can be recognized as such and leave some sort of mark on society; here, in vast "social" space we have inherited, the value of self-disclosure may be solely in the limited recognition it affords us.

Post-Democratic Participation   111

12 While voting is typically done in secret, its culmination in a count functions as an amalgamated expression. Thus, even if one knows one's side will lose, it is important to signal to those who share your preferences that they are not alone.
13 Recently, a number of thinkers including Judith Butler, David Wallace McIvor, and Simon Stow have turned their attention to the political significance of mourning, conceptualizing it as an activity with the power to heal and redefine community relationships. See Butler 2004, McIvor 2016, and Stow 2016. To the extent these activities are able to achieve these goals, they could also constitute political activities; however, to the extent that their ability to influence sovereign decision-making may be overstated, they would still constitute a form of (pseudo-) political activity.
14 Some may characterize these actions as political in themselves, a way of changing outcomes, but while they certainly have effects, they still fall far below the level of sovereign power.
15 One could even be an identitarian—white nationalist or otherwise—post-democrat, depending on how one construes *who* ought to constitute the demos that remains, at present, conspicuously absent.
16 Hayek 2011, p. 166
17 In fact, the very practice of asking large groups of people about their political preferences would seem specific to a democratic outlook toward politics, one which assumes that it matters (politically, at least) whether ordinary citizens can describe themselves as having a coherent set of political preferences.
18 For instance, Hahrie Han argues against the idea that political actors must be politicized before participation, instead arguing that many become politicized through it. See Han 2009.
19 See also Green 2016, ch. 4
20 See Williams 2005, Geuss 2005, 2008, and 2014.
21 Williams 2005, pp. 1–17
22 Williams 2005, p. 2

References

Adorno, Theodor. *Minima Moralia.* New York: Verso Press, 2005.
Arendt, Hannah. *The Human Condition.* Chicago: University of Chicago Press, [1958] 1998.
Butler, Judith. *Precarious Life: The Powers of Mourning and Violence.* New York: Verso Press, 2004.
Foucault, Michel. *The History of Sexuality, Vol. 3: The Care of the Self.* New York: Random House, 1986.
Geuss, Raymond. *Outside Ethics.* Princeton, NJ: Princeton UP, 2005.
Geuss, Raymond. *Philosophy and Real Politics.* Princeton, NJ: Princeton UP, 2008.
Geuss, Raymond. *A World Without Why.* Princeton, NJ: Princeton UP, 2014.
Green, Jeffrey. *The Shadow of Unfairness: A Plebeian Theory of Liberal Democracy.* New York: Oxford UP, 2016.
Han, Hahrie. *Moved to Action: Motivation, Participation, and Inequality in American Politics.* Stanford, CA: Stanford UP, 2009.
Hayek, Friedrich. *The Constitution of Liberty.* Chicago: The University of Chicago Press, 2011.
McIvor, David W. *Mourning in America: Race and the Politics of Loss.* Ithaca, NY: Cornell UP, 2016.

Smith, Daniel. "It's the End of the World as We Know It … And He Feels Fine." *The New York Times Magazine*, April 17th, 2014. Web. <https://www.nytimes.com/2014/04/20/magazine/its-the-end-of-the-world-as-we-know-it-and-he-feels-fine.html>. Accessed July 22, 2019.

Stow, Simon. *American Mourning: Tragedy, Democracy, and Resilience.* New York: Cambridge UP, 2016.

Williams, Bernard. *In the Beginning was the Deed.* Princeton, NJ: Princeton UP, 2005.

Zizek, Slavoj. *The Sublime Object of Ideology.* New York: Verso Press, 1989.

7

CONCLUSION

Despite our sympathies, we can no longer afford to think like democrats. We must begin to take seriously the pervasive conditions of political powerlessness we find ourselves in. This is not easy, nor is it desirable, much in the same way that confronting the consequences of rampant climate change or nuclear proliferation has become our unwelcome, but necessary task. But we must try, because unless we are willing to either defend the mere fantasy of democratic citizenship or give up on the idea altogether, there is no alternative. We live a post-democratic existence; we should try to do so honestly.

This means, first of all, reconceptualizing what it means to be a citizen under post-democratic conditions. This begins by challenging the idea that mass democracy, at least as it's presently practiced, satisfies the basic democratic principles of either popular sovereignty or political equality, but must continue by seriously reflecting on the implications of that criticism; namely, that most ordinary citizens are, and most likely will continue to be, politically insignificant. In this book, we explored how this realization must upset previously held notions of state legitimacy and political membership, as well as ideas about both the citizen's responsibility to and culpability for the actions of the state and their fellow citizens. Moreover, we examined how the fact of post-democracy required a new approach to the practice of political philosophy, one which broke with democratic assumptions about the ability to exercise political influence, and instead focused on how citizens might endure the rule of others, especially within a persistently democratic political imaginary. In that sense, it constituted a therapeutic approach to political philosophy, one oriented toward improving the well-being of the individual by providing a more coherent and illuminating political self-understanding.

As an example of this approach, the book developed one possible Hobbesian answer to the problem of political powerlessness, one drawn from his account of

114 Conclusion

servitude: an instrumental understanding of the citizen's relationship to the state on the basis that, quite frankly, the citizen has no other option but to accept their domination. This too suggested a limited political attachment toward other citizens, understanding them not as fellow participants in a common political enterprise, but only as similarly dominated. Overall, this Hobbesian reading was intended as an exercise in thinking about the broader implications of political powerlessness, not to overcome them, but to orient oneself in relation to them; to learn to think, as it were, as a servant rather than a Hobbesian subject. In doing so, the hope is that one can begin to work through the political frustration, anxiety, and alienation apparent but still left unaddressed within contemporary mass democracy.

Finally, this book argued that a post-democratic diagnosis required a therapeutic approach to (pseudo-)political participation as well, a way of using the endless opportunities still available within post-democracy for expression, dissent, and discussion to begin to work through, perhaps collectively, both the monumental and more quotidian consequences of political powerlessness. By continuing to engage in (pseudo-)political activity with the aim of reflecting on these consequences and working through the feelings they engender, citizens can break with the soporific fantasy of democratic citizenship. In spite of the persistent invitation to think otherwise, one offered by a hollow, lingering democratic political imaginary, citizens can find a new ethical disposition or subjectivity (whether Hobbesian or otherwise) more appropriate to—and perhaps even beneficial for—a self-aware post-democratic existence. In this, they may find not only a clearer vision of themselves, but each other as well.

INDEX

Abramoff, Jack 6
Achen, Christopher 8, 48–51
Achilles 72
acknowledgment 53–55,
 100–103
activation (civic) *see* mobilization (civic)
Adorno, Theodor 68, 100n4
alienation (political) 15, 61–62, 71–72,
 83, 97, 100–107
Anderson, Benedict 84
Anti-Federalists 4
anxiety (political) 15, 61–62, 71–72,
 97, 100–107
Arendt, Hannah 103n11, 104
Aristophanes 1
Aristotle 1–2, 4, 58, 83
Augustine 47, 63
authoritarianism 13, 22, 25, 27,
 30, 32, 108
aversive democracy 46–47

Balibar, Étienne 5
Bartels, Larry 8, 48–51
Becker, Werner 50
Berlusconi, Silvio 5
Boethius 63, 65
Bodin, Jean 26
Bonaparte, Napoleon 4
Brady, Henry 6
Brexit 44
Bronte, Charlotte 45
Brown University 21

Brown, Wendy 5
Bush, George W. 5, 72n53

Carter, Jimmy 3
Cavell, Stanley 46, 63–64
Cicero 4, 66, 83
civic decline 8–9, 43, 47
Clausewitz, Carl von 54
commonwealth: artificial *see* servant
 (Hobbesian); natural *see* subject
 (Hobbesian)
compartmentalization 99–100
Connolly, William 77
consent 49, 80–82, 85, 87–90, 94
conservatism 107–108
Constant, Benjamin 5
consumers (political) 22–23
Cook, Joanna 52
Crouch, Colin 12–14, 21–23, 27–28,
 42–45
Crow Nation *see* Plenty Coups
culpability (political) 3, 14–15, 33, 35–36,
 93–94, 109
Curley, Edwin 94

Dark Mountain Project *see* Kingsnorth, Paul
Deleuze, Gilles 65
democracy: Aristotelian interpretation of
 1–2; classical doctrine/theory of 48–49;
 culture 3, 28–33; faith in 3, 28–33, 51;
 existence of 28; failure of 23–24, 105;
 folk theory of 49; history of 4–6; of

116 Index

moments 69–70; plebeian 71; political
logic of 3, 33; traditions of 3, 28–33
democratic idealism 15, 40–48
democratic realism 15, 48–53, 60
Derrida, Jacques 5, 46
Descartes, René 63
Dewey, John 8–9
Dienstag, Joshua Foa 15, 59, 68–70
discussion (political) 105–106
dissent 104–105
domination 77–81, 89; mystification of 87
Downs, Anthony 7
duty *see* responsibility (political)
Dye, Thomas 6

elite domination 6–7, 9–11, 23, 41,
44, 77
Emerson, Ralph Waldo 63
Entman, Robert 9, 13
environmental activism *see* Kingsnorth,
Paul
Epictetus 66
Epicurus 59, 71
equality (political) 24–26, 50–51
Ercan, Selen 24
ethical self-conception 65–67, 100–103
European Union 11, 21, 23, 42, 44
extrapoliticism 15, 59, 71–72

false consciousness *see* ideology
fear (political) 85–87
Federalism 24
Fishkin, James 9
Fonte, John 21
Foucault, Michel 66–67, 69, 100–101
French Revolution 4
Freud, Sigmund 64, 68
frustration (political) 15, 61–62, 71–72,
97, 100–107
fugitive democracy 52–53, 70

Gagnon, Jean-Paul 24
Gauthier, David 81
Geuss, Raymond 107, 109
Gilens, Martin 7
Glass, James 65–66
gothic reading of democracy 45–46
Green, Jeffrey 15, 25, 59, 71–72, 109
Guattari, Felix 65

Habermas, Jurgen 14, 21, 23, 42–45,
50, 104
Hamas 5

Hampton, Jean 82n21
Hansen, John Mark 10
Hayek, Friedrich 108
Hegel, G. W. F. 5
Heidegger, Martin 63, 65
Hobbes, Thomas 15, 26, 34, 55, 72,
76; comparison of subject and servant
82–88; on culpability 93–94; on
legitimacy 88–89; on membership 90–91
on responsibility 91–92; relevance to
post-democracy 79–82, 114
Honig, Bonnie 45–48
Hook, Sidney 41
hope: political 85–87; radical 68
Hume, David 59–61, 80
Humean citizen 59–61
hyper-democracy 27–28

identity (political) 30–31, 60, 67, 84,
103–104, 108
ideology: false consciousness 29–30;
ideological fantasy 30–33, 48, 70, 81,
88, 98; enjoyment of 32
instrumental approach to sovereignty
90–93
International Criminal Court (ICC)
21, 23

Jacobins 4
Jung, Carl 65

Keynesian economics 28
Kierkegaard, Soren 63, 65
Kingsnorth, Paul 15–16, 97–98,
100–102, 105
Klein, Naomi 100

Lear, Jonathan 15, 67–69
legitimacy (political) 3, 14–15, 33–34,
51, 88–89, 109
liberalism 5, 34, 51n41, 69, 91
liberty 5, 62, 80, 80n14, 82, 86
lobbying 6–7, 24, 43
Locke, John 81

Machiavelli, Niccolò 54, 109
Madison, James 4
Mann, Thomas 7
Marcuse, Herbert 65
Marsilius of Padua 4
Martel, James 28
Marx, Karl 1, 5, 41, 64
Maurier, Daphne du 45

Index **117**

mechanic (Aristotelian) 1–2, 58
membership (political) 3, 14–15, 33–35, 90, 109
Michels, Robert 48
Mikucka, Malgorzata 8
Mill, John Stuart 5, 50
mobilization (civic) 10
Montaigne, Michel de 63
Mosca, Gaetano 48
Mouffe, Chantal 27

Nietzsche, Friedrich 35, 47, 63, 65, 68
noble lie 30, 51
Norris, Andrew 64
Norval, Aletta J. 46–48

obligation *see* responsibility (political)
Ochlocracy 4
Odysseus 85
oligarchy 3–4, 11–12, 22, 24, 32–34
Ornstein, Norman 7
Otanes 72

Page, Benjamin I. 7
Pareto, Vilfredo 48
perfectionism 47
Pericles 24
pessimism (philosophical) *see* Dienstag, Joshua Foa
Peterman, James 63–64
Pettit, Philip 77–78, 80, 90
Plato 4, 72
Plenty Coups 15, 67–68
Political expression 103–104
political realism 98, 107, 109–110
popular sovereignty 24–26, 50–52
post-democracy: acknowledgement of 41, 53–55; definition of 11–14, 22–24, 32–33; history of 21–22; political logic of 88–95; problem of 33–36, 40–41, 43–44, 48, 51–55;
post-politics 27
powerlessness *see* post-democracy: problem of
Prior, Markus 9
property 4, 34, 90
(pseudo-)political practice 14, 55, 97, 102–109
public opinion 6, 13, 22–23, 29, 32n39 79n8
Putnam, Robert 8

quietism (political) 108

Rancière, Jacques 13–14, 21–23, 27–28, 32n39, 52–53
Rawls, John 91
Reich, Robert 8, 10
responsibility (political) 3, 14–15, 33, 35, 91–93, 109
Rorty, Richard 14, 21, 23, 42–45
Rosenstone, Steven 10
Rousseau, Jean-Jacques 5, 63, 65, 68

Sarracino, Francesco 8
Schattschneider, E. E. 9–10, 48–49, 52
Schier, Steven 10
Schlozman, Kay 6
Schmitt, Carl 26
Schopenhauer 68
Schumpeter, Joseph 25, 48
Seneca, 66–67
servant (Hobbesian): connection to post-democratic fear 87–88; connection to post-democratic political logic 88–95; contrast with subject 79–85; definition 79–80
shareholder democracy 22
Shklar, Judith 34
Sigwart, Hans-Jorg 93
Sitting Bull 67
Skocpol, Theda 8, 10–11
slave (Hobbes) 82, 90
Socrates 62–63, 65
South African Truth and Reconciliation Committee 47
Steuernagel, Gertrude 65–66
Strauss, Leo 86
subject (Hobbesian): connection to democratic hope 85–87; contrast with servant 79–85; definition 79
subjectivity, crisis of 66–68, 101–102
Supreme Court (US) 24

Tacitus 66
therapeutic approach: to philosophy 62–66; to political activity 16, 55, 101–103, 106–109; to political philosophy 15, 55, 58–59, 76
Thoreau, Henry David 34, 63
Thucydides 109
Tocqueville, Alexis de 5, 21
Twitter 29
Tzu, Sun 54

118 Index

United Nations (UN) 21

Verba, Sidney 6
Violence: of founding 80–82, 85
    legitimate 26

War of 1812 4
Weber, Max 26, 48, 68, 77
Welch, Stephen 27

William of Ockham 4
Williams, Bernard 107, 109–110
Willis, Andre 42
withdrawal 99–100, 108
Wittgenstein, Ludwig 63
Wolin, Sheldon 14, 21–22, 52–53
World Bank 21

Zizek, Slavoj 27, 30–31, 98–99